TRE
FO
ARK

GW01316104

Scottish Reformation Society
Academic Series :: Volume 2

Scottish Reformation Society
Academic Series :: Volume 2

General Editors:
DOUGLAS SOMERSET AND MATTHEW VOGAN

The Society also publishes *The Scottish Reformation Society Historical Journal.* The aim of the journal is to publish 'original scholarly articles, written from an evangelical perspective, on subjects connected with Scottish Church history'.

TREMBLING
FOR THE
ARK OF GOD

James Begg and
The Free Church of Scotland

JAMES W. CAMPBELL

British Library Cataloguing in Publication Data

ISBN 978-0-9500319-6-5

© James W. Campbell 1980

Published in 2011
by the
Scottish Reformation Society
The Magdalen Chapel, 41 Cowgate, Edinburgh EH1 1JR

www.scottishreformationsociety.org.uk

The Scottish Reformation Society is a charity registered in Scotland.
No: SC007755

Printed by Lulu.com

Contents

Preface

THE purpose of the Scottish Reformation Society Academic Series is to make certain contemporary academic works available to the wider public. The works in mind are those which examine aspects of Scottish Church history, or related matters, from a perspective sympathetic to Protestantism and Evangelicalism. There is a dearth of such writing at present, and what there is does not find a ready publisher. It is hoped that the Series will stimulate research in areas of evangelical interest and will help to counter the anti-Protestant spirit that is all too common in Scottish academic circles. Contributors to the Series are allowed reasonable academic liberty in the views that they express, and the Scottish Reformation Society is not to be seen as endorsing every opinion and detail.

This volume consists of an M.Th. thesis on James Begg, originally submitted to Westminster Theological Seminary in 1980. It has been lightly revised for the present publication. The thesis shows, in brief compass, what a remarkable man James Begg was. His ecclesiastical opponents portrayed him as narrow-minded and old-fashioned, but, as is seen here, his aims were broader, more enlightened, and vastly more biblical, than theirs were.

This publication is of special interest because Begg was one of the founders of the Scottish Reformation Society, and was for many years the editor of its magazine *The Bulwark*.

Douglas Somerset
Matthew Vogan
General Editors
Scottish Reformation Society
Academic Series

Introduction

MY introduction to James Begg as a figure of importance to Scottish Church History came upon reading the *History of the Free Presbyterian Church of Scotland*. In that work his name was mentioned many times, usually with an important quotation from a speech or writing. Further investigation revealed almost nothing about the man. The other leaders of the Free Church in that period were well known to students of Scottish history, with Robert Rainy the chief among them. Writers of this century have been more than willing to include the victors in the battles of that era among the worthies of Scottish Church History, but little that was positive has been said of Begg.

It appeared to me to be a matter of some significance to examine the writings of this man, recognized in his day as a leader of the Free Church, but relegated by modern students of the period to that state of limbo which is reserved for Puritans, Calvinists, and others of such ilk. This thesis makes no pretense to greatness; certainly much more might be done to honor the memory of James Begg, but at least some time and effort has been spent considering the published writings of one who gave greatly of his time and effort to the Cause of Christ.

Beyond any obligation to Begg himself, there is the interest inherent in the controversies themselves. At least half of this thesis is devoted to Begg's defense of the Establishment Principle in the Free Church of Scotland. This is not an issue which seems to be of great importance in Reformed circles today. And yet can it be that all the questions have been answered? The revisions to the Westminster Confession made at the time of the American Revolution are taken by many to be the final word on the subject. But does this do away with the need to talk of the Establishment Principle, of the duty which the state receives from God Himself to support the Church of Jesus Christ? A study of this controversy in the nineteenth century Free Church may enable modern Reformed Christians to recognize principles which are worthy of support in our day. We may live in a post-Christian, certainly post-Constantinian era, but is that a result of forces so much bigger than we that they cannot be contested? Is it not just as possible that our present circumstances are the result of lethargy and lack of concern for that social responsibility so evidenced in the career of James Begg?

A final reason for my interest in Begg is a concern with the Free Church of Scotland itself in that period. The move from Chalmers, Cunningham and Duncan to Rainy and his party is a short one in terms of time, but a very great one in terms of allegiance to confessional standards. How did the Free Church decline so rapidly? What caused such a shift in principles? Obviously the answer to these questions involves more than a study of James Begg alone, but a look at his career may serve as a way of approaching the analyzer at least. Can it be that the Free Church declined from Reformed orthodoxy not so much because of the power of those who attacked the standards of the past, but because of the impotency of those who defended these standards? Does James Begg show us, therefore, not merely personal tragedy as he struggled against all comers, cause after cause, only to have his whole agenda go down to defeat after his death, but also the tragedy of the Free Church itself, which basked in the glow of a unity and strength in 1843 which proved to be only a mask hiding basic divisions? If we are ever to understand the history of this period, we must begin to consider not only the attractive figures who appeal to modern churchmen and historians but also those individuals who seem out of place to modern ideas and customs, men like Begg who, in the race of what he considered to be false ideas, false promises, false men, trembled for the Ark of God and rose to its defense.

April 1980

After thirty one years, I am still impressed by the work of James Begg. Standing for the truth is never easy. Begg ought to be an example to all who would seek to honor the Lord Jesus in thought, word, and deed. I offer my thanks to the Scottish Reformation Society for publishing my thesis and especially to Simon Padbury and Douglas Somerset for seeing my original manuscript, produced on a portable typewriter in 1980, into an age of digital wonders.

JAMES W. CAMPBELL
North Haven, Connecticut
August 2011

Biographical Note

BEGG did not keep a Journal later to be published by an admiring student. Little by way of correspondence has been compiled. His biographer, Thomas Smith, although well-intentioned, did not produce a great work, although the first 113 pages of the first volume were actually written by Begg as the start of an autobiography. C.H. Spurgeon speaks of this two-volume biography as the case of "a man buried beneath a pyramid of documents."[1] The facts of his life can be quickly stated.[2]

Begg was born in 1808 in New Monkland, Lanarkshire, where his father served as parish minister. He was proud of his ancestors and their allegiance to the Covenant. The following paragraph from Begg's autobiographical notes shows his affection for the worthies of the past and serves as a description of his own determination to stand firm for Christ.

> The people of New Monkland sent a detachment of men to the battle of Bothwell Bridge, John Man, elder, Ballochnie, being the standard-bearer. He carried a handsome yellow silk banner emblazoned

---

1. C.H. Spurgeon, *Autobiography, Volume II, The Full Harvest* (Edinburgh: The Banner of Truth Trust, 1973), p. xi.

2. See the articles on Begg in the *Dictionary of National Biography* and *Fasti Ecclesiae Scoticanae.*

with inscriptions and emblems in gold, which is still preserved by his descendents, and which I have often seen – indeed, which I got some time ago repaired. The principal motto on the flag is, "East Monkland for Church and State, According to the Word of God and the Covenant," and there is the representation of a Bible, a crown and thistle, with the motto, *Nemo me impune lacessit*, and under it a hand grasping a drawn dagger.[3]

Begg was educated at the University of Glasgow and was licensed as a preacher in 1829 after studying with Thomas Chalmers in Edinburgh. During his student days, controversy raged in Edinburgh concerning the proposal for Roman Catholic Emancipation. Chalmers and Andrew Thomson, important figures in Begg's life as a student, were in favor of the liberal proposals. Begg declared that these two men were "the main agents, under the Divine blessing of turning the tide in Scotland in favour of evangelical religion",[4] but he was willing to stand against them along with such leaders as Thomas M'Crie and Begg's own father who were opposed to the new measures. From the start of his career, therefore, Romanism was seen as a great threat and the nature of the Protestant response to it a matter of great concern. Begg might admire Chalmers and Thomson but he was not afraid to disagree with them.

> ... the Church has ever since been sinking into deeper apathy on the subject of Romanism, and now a disastrous crisis seems near. This very apathy has in no small measure been owing to the elaborate efforts

---

3. Thomas Smith, *Memoirs of James Begg, D.D., Minister of Newington Free Church, Edinburgh.* (Edinburgh: James Gemmell, 1885 & 1888), vol. I, p. 2.
4. Ibid., p. 62.

made at the time to which I refer to persuade the people of the United Kingdom that Popery had essentially changed, and that the safeguards and other efforts in defense of Protestant truth and liberty found necessary in the days of our ancestors might now be disposed with.[5]

Following his licensing, Begg served in North Leith and Maxweltown. He was ordained to the ministry by the Presbytery of Dumfries in 1830. Serving briefly as assistant at Lady Glenorchy's Chapel in Edinburgh, he became minister of the Middle Parish of Paisley in 1831. Begg was called to the Liberton parish near Edinburgh in 1835 where he remained until the great events of 1843, when he left for the Newington Free Church, serving as minister there until his death.

It appears that Begg supported the evangelical party from the start of his career, and opposed the encroachments of the State in matters ecclesiastical. His first speech in the General Assembly of the Church of Scotland included the following:

> But I have no fear of civil interference. Indeed, a question for every honest man to determine [is] how long he could consistently remain a member of a Church thus rendered unable to enforce its most salutary laws.[6]

The debate was in 1832 and the issue was the matter of overtures before the Assembly regarding calls to the ministry. The details of the debate are not important, but it should be noted that James Begg was prepared as early as this date to consider leaving the Church of Scotland.

---

5. Ibid., p. 76.
6. Ibid., p. 239.

As a Free Church minister, Begg was involved in much of the life of the new denomination. He was elected moderator of the General Assembly in 1865 and served on committees of the Assembly many times, particularly the important committees on Church Union and the Housing Question.

Begg's involvement in other organizations will be mentioned below when his work for better housing for the working class is considered. He did work with the Building Society of Edinburgh and a section of its housing developments is still called "Begg's Buildings."

Always interested in popularizing the theological and ecclesiastical issues of the day, he was a founder of the Scottish Reformation Society and editor of its publication, *The Bulwark*. He also edited *The Watchword*, a Journal devoted to the conservative position within the Free Church.

Possibly his most dramatic role in the courts of the Free Church occurred in 1878 during the trial of W. Robertson Smith. It was in response to Begg's remark that many in Scotland trembled for the Ark of God, that Smith was able to respond and used the term "worldly ecclesiastic" which many took to be in reference to James Begg.

Begg travelled often in Scotland and England, particularly in support of his housing goals. In 1844-45, he visited Canada on behalf of the Free Church, and also traveled to the United States, where he preached before Congress. In 1874, he visited India, New Zealand, Australia and Ceylon. He died in 1883.

TREMBLING
FOR THE
ARK OF GOD

*"The hearts of the best people in Scotland
are trembling for the Ark of God."*
JAMES BEGG

Debate in the Free Church General Assembly, 1878

Chapter I

THE CONSTITUTION OF THE FREE CHURCH OF SCOTLAND

The Establishment Principle and its place in the Scottish Church

THE Establishment Principle can be defined as "the duty of the State to recognize the Church of Christ."[1] Obviously, such recognition might take many forms and therefore precise definitions are required. That process of defining the relations between the Church and the State can be understood to be the major theme of much of the history of Scotland in the seventeenth century. The official formulation of the principle is found in the Westminster Confession of Faith, in particular chapters XXIII and XXXI. The Confession was adopted by the General Assembly of the Church of Scotland at Edinburgh, August 27, 1647, but even at the moment of adoption something more had to be said by the Assembly. There was a danger of misunderstanding the Confession as it related to the power of the civil magistrate in the calling of Church councils. The Assembly declared that the provi-

---

1. *History of the Free Presbyterian Church of Scotland*, 1893-1970. (Inverness: J.G. Eccles, no date), p. 374.

sions which called upon the magistrate to organize assemblies of the Church was to be understood as being in reference to "Kirks not settled, of constituted in point of government."[2] So, too, the Assembly re-affirmed that dearly bought right,

> ... it being also free to assemble together synodically, as well *Pro re nata* as at the ordinary times, upon delegation from the churches, by the intrinsical power received from Christ, as often as it is necessary for the good of the Church so to assemble ...[3]

With this clarification, the Confession became the doctrinal standard of the Church of Scotland and the debate over the Establishment Principle since that time has been in its essentials a discussion of the Westminster standards.

In order to show the place given to the Establishment Principle in the time of James Begg and his defense of it as a Free Church Principle, three writers will be considered, Robert Shaw (1845), William Cunningham (1851), and James Bannerman (1869).

Shaw in his commentary on the Confession of Faith, asserted at the start of his examination of Chapter XXIII, that,

> the Sacred Scriptures are a perfect "rule of faith and manners." They prescribe the duty incumbent upon men in every station and relations, whether members of the Church of the Commonwealth – whether as rulers or as subjects. Any summary of Christian doctrine, therefore, which did not exhibit the duty of civil rulers, especially in reference to religion and the kingdom of Christ, would be extremely defective.[4]

---

2. Publications Committee of the Free Presbyterian Church of Scotland, *The Confession of Faith* ... (Inverness: Eccleslitho, 1970), p.15.

3. Ibid.

4. Robert Shaw, *The Reformed Faith*. (Inverness: John G. Eccles, 1974), p, 241.

Shaw recognized that there were many in the history of the Christian Church who did not agree with such a statement. He named the Anabaptists of the sixteenth century and the English Sectaries of the Westminster Assembly period.

It was not against such opponents alone that the Confession had to speak; there was also the opposite danger of Erastianism. Shaw understood this chapter of the Confession as guarding against both of these errors.

> In opposition to Erastian principles ... they declare that the magistrate may not take upon himself either the ministerial dispensation of the Word and sacraments, of any part of the government of the Church ... yet, to guard against the other extreme, they assert, in opposition to the Sectarians of that age, that it is his duty to employ his influence and authority, in every way competent to him, for the good of the Church, and the advancement of the interests of true religion.[5]

Such rather general statements by Shaw were spelled out in greater detail by William Cunningham in an article written in 1851, but published posthumously in his *Discussions on Church Principles* in 1863. Cunningham recognized three possible theories regarding the relationship of Church and State.

The first of these is found in the doctrine of the Church of Rome, which claims "the superiority in point of jurisdiction of the church over the state – the right of the ecclesiastical rulers to exercise authoritative Control in civil matters."[6]

---

5. Ibid., p. 245.

6. William Cunningham, D.D., *Discussions on Church Principles*. (Edinburgh: T. & T. Clark, 1863), p. 201.

Similar to the claims of Rome, in that one of the two institutions was advanced to a position of superiority, was the doctrine usually called Erastianism, which states "the superiority of the State over the church, or the right of the civil rulers to exercise jurisdiction in ecclesiastical affairs."[7]

The third theory denies both the Popish and Erastian claims and maintains instead that,

> the Church and the State are two co-equal independent powers each supreme in its own distinct province and neither having any authoritative control over the other.[8]

It is this third alternative, according to Cunningham, which is enshrined in the Westminster Standards.

It is interesting that Cunningham does not mention as an alternative the Voluntary Principle. It would appear to be the case that in spite of the heated controversy which was about to develop in the Free Church in the next decade, as yet in 1851 Voluntaryism was not considered as an alternative equal in importance to the other three. Ian R. Tallach, in a fine modern summary of the Establishment Principle, has added the Voluntary theory to Cunningham's list of three, defining it as an approach which recognizes the distinction between the Church and the State, but denies that there can be any legitimate conjunction of their sovereign spheres.[9]

---

7. Ibid., p. 207.

8. Ibid.

9. Ian R. Tallach, "God's Church in Relation to the State," *The Bulwark* (November/December 1979): 8, 9.

James Bannerman, in his two-volume work *The Church of Christ*, presented what may be the most elaborate and definitive exposition of Scottish Reformed theology in regard to this doctrine. Having asserted the distinction and independence of Church and State, Bannerman proceeded to consider the lawfulness, duty and necessity of their connection. Voluntaryism was by 1869 a matter of major concern to the Free Church and Bannerman devotes over fifty pages to its refutation. While it is not necessary to examine Bannerman's argument in detail for purposes of this paper, his position in regard to the duty of maintaining the Church-State connection is worthy of note. This provides something of a theoretical foundation for the more polemical work of James Begg which will be examined in detail below.

Writing as a Free Churchman, Bannerman distinguished first between the *recognition* of the Church on the part of the State and the *maintenance* of the Church by the State. In an argument which was to be used by Begg also, Bannerman showed that the duty of recognition is a duty incumbent upon the State at all times. To go beyond this recognition to the level of actual endowment may or may not be incumbent upon the State, depending upon circumstances.[10] With such a distinction in mind, Bannerman advanced the following principles which assert the duty of the State and the Church to maintain such a connection.

I. The first principle, then, which I lay down is, that both the state and the Church are to be accounted moral parties responsible to God.[11]

---

10. James Bannerman, *The Church of Christ*. (Edinburgh: The Banner of Truth Trust, 1974), vol. I, pp. 124-125.

11. Ibid., p.126.

The State as well as the Church is a moral institution. By this Bannerman meant that categories of right and wrong can be applied to the State, it is responsible to God for its actions. He rejected the argument which suggests that only individuals are responsible and that when such individuals are organized into a society responsibility ceases. Such an argument cannot hold when speaking of a voluntary, humanly contrived society or club, according to Bannerman, certainly therefore it cannot be applied to an institution which is established in accordance with the command of God.

> **II.** The second position that I lay down is, that both the Church and state, in consequence of this responsibility to God, are bound to own and recognize His revealed word.[12]

The second principle is a corollary of the first. Such a teaching is denied by the advocates of the Voluntary Principle which asserts that the State, as an institution, has nothing to do with religion and is bound to maintain a neutral position regarding Christianity. Such a teaching is nothing short of a denial of the State's responsibility as a moral institution to God. Bannerman argues to the contrary:

> As the moral creature of God – more especially as His express ordinance, – the civil magistrate of the state is responsible to Him; and because responsible, is bound in its place, and according to its nature, to own and recognize His revealed will.[13]

> **III.** The third position that I lay down is, that the state, by a regard to itself, and to the very objects for which it exists as a state, is bound

---

12. Ibid., p. 128.
13. Ibid., p. 130.

to recognize the true religion, and, so far as it is in its power, to promote its interests.[14]

The State, as a moral institution, examining the Word of God, and finding there direction for its task, must see that the Word clearly identifies the interests of civil society with the interests of true religion. So, too, the Word teaches, according to Bannerman, that the State, seeking to achieve its goal of the greatest good for the society, must turn to the Gospel as the only answer to society's greatest need.

> **IV.** The fourth position that I lay down is, that the state is bound, by a regard to the Church, as God's ordinance for good, to countenance it, and, so far as it is in its power, to advance its interests.[15]

The State is required not only to support Christian principles in regard to matters of concern to the State, but to support the Church of Christ itself. Bannerman argued that there were many ways in which the State could support the Church without danger of encroachment upon the character or rights of either. These included the protection of the law for the Church that it might be free to exercise its functions in the society. The State might recognize the truth of scripture by adding to civil law various provisions of the divine, such as the observation of the Sabbath Day. Various forms of financial aid might be offered to the Church by the State, including the endowment of churches and provision for the salaries of ministers.

> **V.** The fifth position that I lay down is, that the duty of the state thus to recognize, and, in so far as circumstances permit, to endow

---

14. Ibid.
15. Ibid., p. 131.

the Church, is undeniably countenanced by the whole tenor of Scripture.[16]

Bannerman taught that the whole of scripture supported the view of Church-State relations expressed above. The Old Testament taught of an alliance between Church and State which he understood to be of a permanent nature, although many specific aspects of it were ceremonial and peculiar to those ancient times. This alliance, while not evidenced in the actual practice of the New Testament for obvious reasons, nevertheless is to be maintained by the Church, for there is no evidence at all of the repeal of such an ordinance.

To Bannerman, this was the strongest evidence of all for the present character and practice of the Christian Church. The duty of such a connection, of such a biblical alliance, can be summarized as follows:

> We find the whole tenor of Scripture bearing testimony to the duty and responsibility of the state in the matter, and lending not a contradiction but a confirmation to the dictates of nature and reason, which declare that nations and communities, like the individuals that compose them, are the subjects of Christ, and as such bound to bring their honour and glory to His church.[17]

This, then, was the theological foundation for the work of James Begg. The Westminster Confession as it had been taught and interpreted by Scottish divines for two hundred years argued for the Establishment Principle. Men such as Shaw, Cunningham and

16. Ibid., p. 133.
17. Ibid., pp. 134-135.

Bannerman had made the case clear. But Scotland and its Free Church were about to undergo an intensive debate concerning this principle. It was to be as if such works had never been written. By the 1860's such had been forgotten in Scotland concerning her own traditions and standards. A new wind was blowing across the land. It was a strong wind, prepared to uproot the old landmarks. Such a day required strong leaders, who were willing to endure great criticism and to be considered out of date and old fashioned. Although hardly friends to the views of James Begg, Drummond and Bulloch, writing in the 1970's recognize that this was a strange state of affairs and summarize it in this fashion.

> ... Begg maintained within the Free Church the Calvinist tradition that it was essential for the Church, not merely to succour the casualties of society, but to uphold a just social order. So far was the tradition forgotten that his opponents sneered at his outlook as a combination or theological conservatism and political radicalism, but in each he represented the outlook of an older Scotland.[18]

The Voluntary Controversy in the Free Church – Details of the Conflict

In the broadest sense, the Voluntary Controversy was a matter of concern to the Free Church of Scotland from 1860 until 1900. The periods from 1863-1873, 1873-1886, and 1890-1900 can be seen as times when the controversy focused upon particular concerns. The first of these, 1863-1873, is the most important for purposes of this paper, for in it James Begg played a prominent role. It involved a debate and growing division within the Free Church

---

18. A.L. Drummond and James Bulloch, *The Church in Victorian Scotland 1843-1874*. (Edinburgh: The Saint Andrew Press, 1975), p. 134.

over the question of union with the United Presbyterian Church, a professed voluntary body which rejected the orthodox views of the establishment of religion in Scotland. The often complicated debates of this era in ecclesiastical politics will be detailed below.

The second period, 1873-1886, is directly related to the first. The question was still that of the lawfulness of the establishment of religion, but the specific cause of the debate within the Free Church was the proposed disestablishment of the Church of Scotland. Generally, this was a time of anti-establishment feeling in Scotland, England and Ireland, and the tide of public opinion swept up those who might appear to be beyond its reach in a non-established Church. Begg was involved in this debate, too, and he expressed concern not merely with events in Scotland but with anti-establishment moves throughout the United Kingdom.

The third period, 1890-1900, is beyond the interest of this paper since Begg did not live to see these dark days for his Church, party, and establishment views. The debate in this decade was over the legality and propriety of a Declaratory Act which would free ministers and elders of the Free Church from both doctrinal and constitutional ties with the past. It was the passage of such an act by the Free Church which was to lead to the formation of the Free Presbyterian Church in 1893 and finally, with union achieved, the Continuation of the "Wee Frees" in 1900. Mention will be made of the details of this period of the controversy only in passing.

It is important to outline the details of the first of these periods because an analysis of Begg's thought and tactics must keep the practical political questions of the day in mind. Begg wrote much by way of controversial material and little of a detached, academic nature. He was a man of his time and it was the debates of his time which brought forth his literary effort.

In 1863 the General Assemblies of the Free Church and the United Presbyterian Church appointed committees to consider the possible union of the two denominations. From the start, it was obvious that important questions had to be dealt with. The procedure to be followed by the committees was one which brought to the forefront the issues upon which there was significant difference of opinion. In particular, the questions of the Church-State relationship and the extent of doctrinal agreement were noted as matters which needed to be resolved before union could occur.[19] All of this was to state the obvious. It was not a matter of some small disagreement on a minor point or two; there was outright contradiction between the views of the two churches at least in regard to the Establishment Principle. The United Presbyterian Church opposed the establishment of religion and the Free Church supported it, at least in principle. This at least was clear. But there was also some concern regarding doctrinal matters. The suggestion was made that all was not right in the United Presbyterian view of the atonement. The Double Reference theory of the atonement had been put forward in the Secession Church and it was clear to some in the Free Church that the United Presbyterians had not disowned it.[20]

In the light of these problems and with the conviction that nothing should be given away in the course of negotiations, the

---

19. J.R. Fleming, *The Church in Scotland, 1843-1874*. (Edinburgh: T. & T. Clark, 1927), p. 175.

20. *History of the Free Presbyterian Church*, p. 9.

committee of the Free Church was instructed to remember that "absolute regard should be observed as to the principles of the Free Church of Scotland."[21]

By 1867 matters were moving toward a period of crisis. Articles of Agreement were approved by the two committees. These were an attempt to compromise by stating only the views upon which there was agreement in the two churches. The Articles declared that the Churches were in agreement on the fact that the Civil Magistrate must not interfere with the government of the Church and that it was a perpetual obligation of Christians to support the Church by freewill offerings.[22] These Articles did not mention the question of establishments or endowments and it is clear that, short of excluding the most blatant Erastianism, little is resolved by their formulation.

The meeting of the Free Church General Assembly in 1867 put the work of the committee to its first test. The motion to receive the Articles included in it an expression of satisfaction with the progress made toward agreement on this league and a recognition that "on the question of the Civil Magistrate there appeared to be no bar to the Union contemplated."[23] This was too much for the Constitutional party, as Begg and his followers had begun to be called. The vote on the motion was 346:120 in favor. A number of ministers and elders in the Assembly felt that, however preliminary and moderate its tone, the Articles drawn up by the committee had already gone too far. Four prominent conservatives

---

21. Ibid.
22. Fleming, p. 177.
23. Ibid., p. 179.

resigned from the Free Church committee. This included James Begg who also filed a protest before the General Assembly.[24]

It was apparent that the division within the Free Church of Scotland was growing. There was increased talk of parties and party leaders within the Church, particularly at the meetings of the General Assembly. Both sides began to organize, to publicize their views, to recruit followers, to seek support from officers and members of the Church. In the words of one church historian, "Hitherto anti-unionism had been a tendency, now it was an organization."[25]

The organization of the anti-unionists centered in James Begg, but his was not the only position of leadership among the conservatives. Men such as John Kennedy of Dingwall, George Smeaton, Hugh Martin and Dr Nixon of Montrose provided articulate and powerful leadership for the conservative cause.[26] A monthly journal, *The Watchword*, was organized with Begg as the editor. An intensive pamphlet war was begun with propaganda against the union movement being spread throughout Scotland. In the light of such intensive activities, it became clear that the possibility of a split within the Free Church was a growing reality in the period 1867-1873.[27]

The influence of this anti-union party was greater than its numbers alone might imply. There was also a significant number of what might be considered a middle party, not fiercely against

---

24. G.N.M. Collins, *The Heritage of our Fathers* (Edinburgh: Knox Press, 1974), p. 72.

25. Fleming, p. 180. Quotation from Prof. Carnegie Simpson.

26. *History of the Free Presbyterian Church*, p. 10.

27. Ibid., p. 11.

union, but not willing to move toward union if that involved a split in the Free Church. Fleming suggests that it was this middle party which provided the real source of strength for leaders like Begg in this period, for with these moderate votes added to the anti-unionists opposition to any given issue might be considerable.

> The determining factor which thwarted the Union for the time being was the emergency (*sic*) of a middle party in the Church Assembly that was decidedly adverse to union at the price of rending asunder the Church of 1843, which to them was more sacrosanct than any more comprehensive and more liberal Church could possibly be.[28]

It was the influence of some of these in the middle party which carried great weight in the Free Church, men such as Andrew and Horatius Bonar and A. Moody Stuart. Whatever might be their views on establishments and unions, they opposed the plan for union with the United Presbyterians because they were unwilling to divide the Free Church. With the support of this middle party, the anti-unionists were a force to be reckoned with. In the course of the debate from 1867-1873, they were able to frustrate the supporters of Union time and again, but it is significant that they were never able to gain majorities on any vote in the Assembly. Had the pro-union forces been willing to split the Church, they had the votes to do so.

The anti-unionists attempted to use the courts of the Church, particularly the General Assembly, to achieve their goal of defeating any proposal for union with the Voluntaries. In the Assembly of 1868, fifty-seven overtures hostile to union were presented by

---

28. Fleming, p, 181.

Presbyteries and Synods.[29] The Assembly of 1869 saw an attempt to end all discussion about union with a motion ordering that "no further steps be taken till negotiation can be resumed with due regard to Scriptural principles and the peace of the church."[30] This was defeated.

Professor James Gibson, a leader of the anti-union party, tabled a protest in the 1870 General Assembly which summarizes the Constitutionalists' views of the whole question of the legality of the moves toward union which required any alteration of the existing principles of the Free Church. Fleming describes this protest as follows:

> Before the debate began a protest was tabled by Professor Gibson ... declaring it *ultra vires* of the Assembly to alter, modify, or compromise any of the fundamental or essential doctrines or principles of the Free Church, or to suggest to the Presbyteries the consideration of any such questions, and further declaring that in the taking part in any discussion leading to a decision on such lines they would not be bound thereby, and would be entitled to maintain all their rights and privileges, and to adopt all competent means to obtain redress.[31]

It was clear to all in what direction the Free Church was headed. If union with the United Presbyterians was achieved, the next step would be an appeal to the civil courts for the property of the Free Church on the part of the minority. All this ill feeling came to a head in the General Assembly of 1872. The Union Committee was unable to present the Assembly with an acceptable plan for

---

29. Ibid., p. 182.
30. Ibid.
31. Ibid., p. 183.

union; the power of the constitutionalists was too great for such an extreme measure. But something else might be brought off in its place. In such an atmosphere, the Mutual Eligibility Plan was suggested.

This Plan was a device whereby ministers of the United Presbyterian Church might be received into the Free Church without any formal application for admission to the denomination. The plan was understood to be a less than subtle attempt to achieve union in practice in spite of the objections of the minority in the Free Church to union in principle.[32]

The pro-union party was prepared initially to insist on this limited recognition of the goal of union. This was more than just a tactic on their part, however. The issue was becoming a matter of conscience for both sides.

> ... it was felt by the majority that to refuse to admit Voluntaries into the ministry of the Free Church, even though willing to sign its official documents, was tantamount to making the Establishment Principle a term of office and so rendering untenable the position of those in the Free Church who openly declared that they no longer held it.[33]

It was in opposition to the Mutual Eligibility Plan that the Constitutionalists came as close as they would in this period to leaving the Free Church. Begg obtained legal counsel, the opinions of which were to be published in 1874 as his most important contribution to the literature of the conflict. A hall was rented by the Constitutionalists in Edinburgh prior to the meeting of

---

32. Collins, p. 73.
33. Fleming, p. 185.

the General Assembly in May of 1872, to which the minority might adjourn if their fellowship in the Free Church Assembly was no longer possible.[34] This reminded many of the move by the Evangelicals in 1843 which led to the formation of the Free Church and many of the middle party, whatever their opinions of the Establishment Principle, were brought face to face with the real possibility of another division in the Reformed Church of Scotland.

At this point, a compromise was effected whereby the possibility of admitting United Presbyterians into the Free Church under the terms of the Mutual Eligibility Plan was accepted, but with strict provisions which clearly assumed that those so admitted would be at one with the Free Church in doctrine and in terms of what was considered to be the "unique position" of that Church.[35] It was in many ways a quiet end to ten years of conflict. Few were happy with the stand-off, but at least the Free Church was preserved for the time being. There were to be no further moves toward union for many years. One Free Church leader prophesied that "death will have a good deal to do among us before the set time of union comes."[36]

In the second period of conflict which can broadly be understood as a part of the Voluntary Conflict, the years 1873-1886 saw the debate shift from the specific question of union between the Free Church and United Presbyterian Church to the more general question of the place of establishments in Scotland.

---

34. *History of the Free Presbyterian Church*, p. 11.

35. Collins, p. 73.

36. Ibid.

In the General Assembly of 1877, James Begg and Robert Rainy were the leaders of their respective parties and both spoke at length regarding the six resolutions received from the Synods of the Free Church respecting the disestablishment of the Church of Scotland. Begg's motion was a summary of his position and that of many in the history of Presbyterianism in Scotland:

> The General Assembly, whilst not satisfied with the existing relations between Church and State in Scotland, and deploring the divisions which exist, hold that it is the duty of this Church to maintain firmly the whole principles of the Disruption; and that can only be done in connection with a decided adherence to the universal supremacy of Christ as King of nations as well as King of saints, with the consequent duty of nations to honour and serve Him by recognizing His truth and promoting His cause; whereas, the direct tendency of a policy of mere disestablishment is to subvert the principles of the Reformation and of the Free Church, inasmuch as the abolition of the existing Establishment is advocated, whilst no clear views of national duty are maintained.[37]

Rainy and his party opposed the Continuation of the establishment of the Church of Scotland. He offered a countermotion to that of Begg, stating that:

> ... it was now the duty of the Legislature, while making due provision for life-interests, to terminate the connection of the State with the existing Established Church, and to give facilities for a beneficial adjustment of ecclesiastical matters in Scotland.[38]

---

37. *History of the Free Presbyterian Church*, p. 21.
38. Ibid., p. 22.

The vote was 460 for Rainy's motion and only 78 for that of James Begg. The support for the Establishment Principle in the Free Church of Scotland was by now very poor indeed.

The debate continued at the General Assemblies of 1878 and 1879. In each case eloquent speeches were made and pleas to constitutional and biblical principles were offered. But in all cases the result was the same. Rainy's party was victorious. James Begg and his supporters lost the votes and protested the decisions of the Assemblies. The Free Church of Scotland, confessions and constitutions notwithstanding, was prepared to support the disestablishment of the State Church in no uncertain terms. The majority motion in the Assembly of 1878, made by Dr Adam of Glasgow stated:

> The Assembly, in accordance with the Claim of Right, and the principles which, from the Disruption, this Church has ever held, hereby declare their solemn conviction that the connection subsisting between the Church now established and the State is wholly indefensible, and ought with as little delay as possible to be brought to a termination.[39]

The debate continued into the next decade and although the labor put forth by all concerned resulted in little practical change in regard to the status of the Established Church, the results of the debate within the Free Church itself were marked. The two parties were farther apart than ever by the 1880's. All that was lacking was the opportunity for another disruption and a breaking of ties of fellowship which had already become very strained indeed.

---

39. Ibid., p. 28.

Begg's Opposition to Voluntaries and Unionists

The writings of James Begg which are the subject of concern to this chapter were not academic treatises. They were usually polemical in nature, seeking not so much to analyze as to attack or defend. Often they were transcripts of speeches made in the courts of the Church or at public gatherings. In order to gain an understanding of Begg's thought on the subset of the establishment of religion and the principles of his opposition to the Unionists, one must examine the range of his writings and piece together statements of principle from material which was not intended to be definitive.

Begg's Principles

James Begg was not opposed to the union of the Presbyterian Churches in Scotland, at least in principle. He was a man who had love and respect for the traditions of his Church and nation, and none of his work in opposition to Voluntaryism can properly be understood if his affection for the Scottish Reformed Church and its history is forgotten. Begg expressed his dream of true biblical union many times, but it is nowhere better evidenced than in the following:

> But He who is wonderful in counsel and excellent in working might, after all, be preparing, by that process of breaking to pieces, a more comprehensive and vital union. Some time and sifting may still be necessary; but if, in a way thoroughly consistent and honouring to God's truth, without which union is a conspiracy against truth, the scattered children of the Covenanters, the sons of Erskine, Gillespie, and Chalmers shall be brought to meet around a common centre, and in these days of trouble, and rebuke, and blasphemy, to blend their several protests into one broad standard uplifted on high, and

emblazoned with Christ's crown and covenant, Scotland may again become glorious as in the days of old; nay, her latter end may become better than her beginning.[40]

Such a glorious vision had to deal with the reality of Voluntaryism. Begg recognized that in defending the Church against the Voluntary attack he was not merely dealing with a minor aberration in an otherwise reasonable and proper view of the relationship between Church and State. Here was not an issue of small practical significance, but one of striking importance to the whole of Christ's church. Here the battle had to be waged against all that would seek to overcome the cause of the Gospel. Its origins betrayed its nature according to James Begg:

> Voluntaryism, although very pretentious and aggressive, is in reality, as a matter of any importance, a thing of yesterday, having originated mainly in the French Revolution. However plausible in appearance, it is one of the most dangerous forms of modern infidelity ...[41]

But why is such strong language required? What is at issue between the advocates of Voluntaryism and the defenders of the Establishment Principle? Begg makes clear that the word "infidelity" used in speaking of the Voluntary position is not merely rhetorical exoneration, but rather defines the core of the problem:

> The question at issue, therefore, is a very serious one, and should arouse the consciences of all patriotic Christians. One would imag-

---

40. James Begg, *Free Church Presbyterianism in the United Kingdom: Its Principles, Duties and Dangers.* (Edinburgh: Duncan Grant, 1865), p.10.

41. James Begg, *Voluntaryism Indefensible; or, a Nation's Duty and Right to Profess and Practice Christianity.* (Edinburgh: no date), p.1.

ine, at the same time, that the answer to it was as clear as the question is important. Are nations, as such, under the moral government of God? Are they not moral and accountable? Are they not the subjects of rewards and punishments?[42]

It might be argued that in analyzing the Voluntary position in this manner, by seeing it as infidelity to the Lordship of Christ, Begg was making too much of a peripheral issue. It may be a matter of some interest and concern, but is it one of critical importance, is it one which required a line to be drawn and no retreat allowed? Begg himself was sensitive to this attack on his position, an attack which minimized the significance of the whole issue, and he made his feelings clear regarding the relative importance of the truths involved in the debate:

> Some, however, are ready to say, "But it is an insignificant doctrine; it may be the truth, but it is a very small truth." Now, on the contrary, I am disposed to maintain that it is a very great truth, and that it is interwoven with the whole of Scripture from beginning to end.[43]

Begg addressed the advocates of union and attempted to show the importance of the Establishment Principle, in terms of morals, church government, and theology. The pro-unionist forces in the Free Church argued that this principle was one which could be put aside in the interests of a comprehensive Presbyterian union. Begg was not willing to allow this, because for him Voluntaryism was a matter of great consequence, for it included issues which

---

42. Ibid., p. 3.

43. James Begg, *The Union Question.* (Edinburgh: James Nichol, 1868), p.21.

could not be compromised. It was this analysis of Voluntaryism which colored the whole of his attack upon the unionists.

> In regard to temporal matters, you could not take a single sixpence of your master's goods without dishonestly neglecting your duties as stewards; and are you to take one of the most precious truths of the Word of God, and give it away as part of the public testimony of the Church? Do not say that it is not the principle of the Headship of Christ over the nations. It is an application of that principle ... You are not entitled to take that principle and throw it open for the purpose of bringing about Union, or for any purpose whatsoever. Dr Candlish may dislike the word apostasy; but I say, I would hold myself an apostate, and a gross apostate, from the truth, which I believe as firmly as I do my own existence – the truth for which I have testified all my life long, and for which I intend to testify till I die – I say I should hold myself to be a shameful apostate if I abandoned that principle.[44]

It was this analysis of Voluntaryism as infidelity and apostasy which also enabled Begg to see the division within the Free Church over the Union question for the tragedy that it was. It was the Voluntary controversy which forced the Free Church of Scotland, an institution which should have been standing firm for the Establishment Principle and laboring with all of its power and resources toward the dream of true biblical union, to become "the sad spectacle to the world and to the other Churches of Christendom of a house divided against itself."[45]

---

44. James Begg, *Present Aspect of the Union Question.* (Edinburgh: Ballantine & Co., 1870), pp. 13-14.

45. James Begg, *The Principles, Position, and Prospects of the Free Church of Scotland.* (Edinburgh: Lyon & Gemmell, 1875), p.21.

The spectacle was a sad one indeed. Above all, it was sad to James Begg. Branded in his day as a disrupter of the peace of the Free Church, as a man behind the times who exalted minor issues to positions of major importance, nevertheless Begg had great dreams for the Reformed Church of Scotland. He was not afraid to state his goals, to define his hopes in terms of visible union among the churches. He did so in 1871 in the midst of controversy:

> That all true-hearted Presbyterians are bound to aim at a comprehensive union, not on the ground of false principle and unworthy compromise, but on the basis of Scripture and in accordance with past attainments.[46]

It was this need to qualify the contemplated union as one loyal to scripture and the past attainments of the Scottish Church which was to prove Begg's greatest point of opposition to the pro-union party and the voluntary movement. Voluntaryism was anathema to James Begg because it was in opposition to both aspects of this qualification. It was opposed to scripture. It denied the Crown Rights of the Lord Jesus. But it was also a cause which had to be opposed because it was in conflict with the past attainments of the Reformed Church in Scotland, the Free Church in particular. More will be said below regarding Begg's views on the Establishment Principle as a part of the binding vows of ministerial fellowship within the Free Church, but it should be noted as a part of the analysis of Voluntaryism, that Begg did not believe

---

46. James Begg, *A Violation of the Treaty of Union the Main origin of Our Ecclesiastical Divisions and Other Evils*. (Edinburgh: Johnstone, Hunter & Co., 1871), p. 39.

that one could be a supporter of the Voluntary position on these matters and an office bearer of the Free Church at the same time. In seeking to define the Union question in 1868, Begg stated:

> With my views I cannot understand how ... a man can be a Voluntary and consistently remain a minister or elder in the Free Church.[47]

It was the unique prerogative of the Free Church to speak in support of the Establishment Principle, for it was the Free Church which had suffered for that very principle. In reflecting upon the Ten Years Conflict, Begg remarked:

> ... that conflict itself was connected with an anti-Voluntary struggle, and would have had no meaning – in truth, would have been absurd – if the Church had seen it to be a duty to abandon the advantage of a Church Establishment and all union between Church and State.[48]

It was from the standpoint of this Church, then, that James Begg sought to oppose the Voluntary movement. It was from within this Church that he sought to oppose infidelity to Christ and to Thomas Chalmers. It was from within this Church that he sought to oppose apostasy from the Crown Rights of the Redeemer and the attainments of the Disruption. It was, after all, this Church which was now attacked from within by those who looked to another tradition, to other fathers, to perhaps even another gospel. It was nothing less than a revolution that James Begg opposed, and nothing less than a revolutionary struggle was to ensue. The

---

47. Begg, *Union Question*, p. 7.

48. James Begg, *Memorial with the Opinions of Eminent Counsel in regard to the Constitution of the Free Church of Scotland.* (Edinburgh: Johnstone, Hunter & Co., 1874), p. 10.

Voluntaries had power, and respectability, and public opinion on their side. But James Begg claimed to have something more: the Word of God, and the testimony of His dealings with the Scottish Church and Nation.

It was well for Begg to marshal his strength and organize his allies, for the dangers inherent in Voluntaryism were great indeed. The move toward Voluntaryism was not only a move away from the traditional way of ordering Church-State relations in Scotland, it was more than this; indeed, more dangerous than this. For James Begg, any move toward Voluntaryism was a move toward secularism, worldliness, and atheism. For all their protestations to the contrary, Begg believed that the pro-union spokesmen in the Free Church were advocates of a position which would bring much of the world into the Church of Christ. Nothing less than the Word of God itself was at stake.

> The Struggle now, however, is a natural result of giving up high principles in the Established Church at the time of the Disruption, for if I were prepared to abandon the Word of God as my only rule, I do not see why I should occupy a humble Puritan position after I have abandoned my Puritan principles. Why not make the Church as attractive to human nature as possible, if I am under no restraint from the Word of God?[49]

Secularism struck at the heart of godly civil government no less than at ecclesiastical order. Perhaps it is here that Begg's hatred of the Voluntary position becomes most graphic and obvious. The struggle was not just between conflicting views of the Church-

---

49. Begg, *Free Church Presbyterianism in the U.K.*, p. 34.

State relationship in Scotland, it was not just a matter of the relative strength of various parties in the courts of the Free Church of Scotland, it was not just a matter of differences of opinion concerning the role of the civil government in spiritual and moral affairs; the struggle was far greater than this. Begg saw that, properly understood, the Voluntary Principle was a threat to all godliness, to the great attainments of the Scottish and English Reformations, to civil liberties, to the rule of law, to the freedoms cherished by British subjects to the continuance of Protestantism in the United Kingdom. Whatever the situation in the Free Church, a man like James Begg was required to speak out on such matters, and to carry the serious implications of this threat to their logical conclusion in language which all might understand.

In a fairly restrained manner, Begg described the threat in 1874 as follows:

> Voluntaryism, being a denial of the moral nature and obligation of States, leads directly to national atheism. It confounds the State with the world, forgetting that civil government is a Divine ordinance, and that the civil magistrate is a minister of God unto the people for good. It is questionable whether Popery itself more directly robs Christ of His glory ...[50]

If even Popery itself might be no worse in practice, then the Voluntary threat must have been terrible indeed. Begg was willing to draw the conclusions and state the implications. The personal conflict with Rainy, the debate within the Free Church itself, these were nothing compared with the great matter before

---

50. Begg, *Memorial of Counsel*, pp. 53-54.

James Begg in his campaign against that national atheism called Voluntaryism and all that would come into Scotland with it:

> The overthrow of the Church Establishments therefore ... could not take place without a social revolution, upon the probable results of which all who are interested would do well to reflect in time. But even this would only be the beginning of the mighty national change which some are so recklessly projecting.[51]

While speaking of disestablishment, which Begg saw as merely the logical working out of the Voluntary Principle, not the Principle itself, he suggested six consequences of this social, ecclesiastical, and civil revolution in the United Kingdom:

> Let any one seriously consider what the practical effect of adopting this blasphemous theory would be. Could any blessing be expected upon the land in connection with it? It would, no doubt, at once overthrow the Church Establishments but it would also overthrow the main structure of British law ... It would overthrow the Protestantism of the Throne ... It would set aside the opening of Parliament with prayer in the name of Christ ... It would set aside all care for the purity of the Authorized Version of Scripture ... It would rescind all Sabbath laws ... and all laws in regard to the purity of marriage ... It would annihilate all teaching of the Bible in our National Schools ...[52]

Begg not only painted a picture of great tragedy if the Voluntary movement and its accompanying trend toward secularism were to win out, he also offered an example of this tragedy in progress. Begg saw the civil government of America, without an established

---

51. Begg, *Voluntaryism Indefensible*, p. 6.
52. Ibid., pp. 6-7.

Church, as one open to all of the anti-Christian demands of the secularists. The American scene was a picture of the consistent application of the Voluntary Principle.

> The various points thus indicated are all demanded by the Secularists of America at present, where there is no Established Church; and this is only a consistent application of the Voluntary principle, as every intelligent Voluntary must know.[53]

Begg summarized his conclusions regarding Voluntaryism and its secular threat in words which indicate the magnitude of the conflict with which he was engaged:

> If admitted, it would not only overturn all Established Churches, but the whole existing constitution of Great Britain, interwoven as it is with Christianity, from the Throne downwards, in connection with which so many national blessings have been enjoyed.[54]

Begg's fight for Christ's crown and covenant would have been difficult enough if he had only dealt with the opposition of the secularists, but another agency was at hand, well armed, ready to do battle, allied with the Voluntaries. That agency was the Church of Rome. In Chapter III of this paper, Begg's labors in opposition to Romanism will be considered in detail, but for now it should be noted that, according to James Begg, it was not the secularists alone who stood to benefit should the principles of the Voluntaries be adopted in the United Kingdom.

Begg saw the Protestant Establishment in the United Kingdom as one of the great bulwarks against the Church of Rome. Begg

---

53. Ibid., p.7.
54. Ibid., p. 2.

was certainly not an advocate of the Episcopal system of Church government, but he recognized that, whatever the faults of the Church of England and the Church of Ireland, they were to be preferred to the Church of Rome. Begg had come out in the Disruption of 1843 and was a loyal Free Churchman, but the Church of Scotland, the Church by law established, was a power which would prevent any increase in the power and influence of Romanism in Scottish affairs.

> I am not to shut my eyes to this, that the whole facts of history and the whole present bearing of things, indicate a great danger to this country from the side of Romanism; and that one great security you have under God for arresting the onward progress of Popery is, that you rulers shall stand on the opposite side, and maintain Protestant truth according to the Word of God, and the constitution of this country.[55]

Robert Rainy in the Free Church was not a Romanist. The Voluntaries in the United Presbyterian Church were not Romanists. The advocates of disestablishment in the three kingdoms were not Romanists. But, whether from knowledge or ignorance, they were doing the work of Rome. Begg recognized that his age was one of great danger for Protestant truth and that instead of seeking to defend and shore up the bulwarks against the Romanist attack, the advocates of the Voluntary Principle were working with the enemy, indeed, they were doing his work for him.

> The Voluntary party, after all, are little more than cats' paws, doing the work of Rome. You will find that the Romish Church claims every

---

55. James Begg, *The Proposed Disestablishment of Protestantism in Ireland: Its Bearings upon the Religion and Liberties of the Empire.* (Edinburgh: James Nichol, 1868), p. 21.

shilling of the endowments which are thus to be set aside in connection with the Irish Establishment.[56]

It was not just a matter of Irish endowments. Remove the Protestantism of the British Constitution, and the Church of Rome was prepared to assume power within the Kingdom which would return the land to an age of darkness. The Voluntary Principle was opposed by James Begg because it was clear to him that only Rome would gain the victory if Voluntaryism were to win out.

We have seen that James Begg opposed the Voluntary movement because of its tendency to aid the secularists and the Roman Church. A third reason might be given for his concern with the progress of Voluntaryism. Although Begg was not a Highlander, yet on many issues he came to represent the Highland cause within the Free Church. He had allies in Highlanders such as John Kennedy. His enemies in the Free Church recognized and at times ridiculed his influence in and support from this area of Scotland. It is significant, therefore, that in one of the few references to the Highlands in his writings, he was concerned to defend the Establishment Principle as an effective means of spreading the Gospel in that region. Begg attacked the Voluntaries for their neglect of the Highlands in their scheme for altering the Church-State relationship in Scotland.

After lauding the Highlanders for adherence to the Free Church cause, and lamenting that such loyalty was no longer being rewarded by respect and admiration on the part of the pro-unionists within their own Church, Begg raised the issue of poverty. Here the loyal Free Churchman defended established

---

56. Ibid., p. 13.

religion as a means of providing funds for evangelical work in the Highlands. It was this establishment, to be sure, which in 1843 had caused great suffering for those who stood with the Free Church, but it was to this establishment, nevertheless, which Begg turned to order a scheme for further Highland work.

> Were the Establishment removed, they would be much at the mercy of men in the south, who have little sympathy with their views and feelings, and who even at present in vain disparage their steadfastness and try to overawe them into submission. Their case deserves very special consideration on the part of the Government and of all true patriots now that there is a practical admission that they have suffered for righteousness' sake. Why, in the name of all that is reasonable, propose to sacrifice the public endownments in the Highlands which belong to them, especially when we are attempting ourselves, with little success, to provide very inferior endowment in connection with Free Church Highland charges? If men were even to succeed in their present unworthy crusade, the old enemies of the Presbyterian Church might perhaps again renew their struggle, backed by the power of England, on the ground that we had spontaneously abandoned the Revolution Settlement, against which they had always protested.[57]

Begg's vision of true Presbyterian union, on the basis of what he termed a "reformed and renovated Establishment," [58] is clear from such a statement. He looked to endowed, reformed, established presbyterian Christianity as the great means by which advances might be made in the social, cultural, economic, educational and

---

57. Begg, *Principles, Position, and Prospects*, p. 28.
58. Ibid., p. 30.

spiritual climate of the Highlands. The Voluntaries and the pro-unionists attacked not merely a principle of the Confession of Faith, or a minor issue of ecclesiastical tradition, they attacked the one proven means of effecting the sort of reform which Begg advocated in the Highlands and in the cities of Scotland as well.

Begg opposed the Voluntary movement because of his conclusion that such a movement was a step away from the biblical principle concerning Church-State relations, because of the dangers inherent in it of secularism and Romanism, because of the need for a purified establishment as an instrument of church extension, but also because of his views on the moral and legal obligations incumbent upon those who had made sacred vows and obligations.

Office-bearers of the Free Church of Scotland had obligated themselves to certain well-defined views on a number of important issues in the areas of doctrine, polity, worship, and the Church-State question. Rainy and others might argue that the latter was a matter of small consequence, that to defend the Establishment Principle in the middle of the 19th century was to be hopelessly outdated and reactionary. For Begg such reasoning was unacceptable. He argued for the principle on biblical, confessional and practical grounds, He defended his position by looking at Voluntaryism and suggesting that great dangers would come with it into the land. But he also suggested that those who were the holders of ordained office in the Free Church had an obligation to support the principle of the establishment simply because they had promised to do so. If such officers could no longer maintain such a principle, they need not perjure themselves for an option was available for those who had changed their views. They could leave the Free Church. Begg himself was willing to leave the Free Church if it required him to deny his solemn vows, and he was not unwilling to suggest such a route to others.

> If any office-bearers of the Free Church, therefore, hold the abstract theory of Voluntaryism, or even make light of it, they ought at once to retire from our communion.[59]

Begg insisted that the standards of the Free Church required such an absolute statement. As will be examined below, his most extended contribution to the literature of the debate was his *Memorial of Counsel* of 1874 which pursued the argument exhaustively. But throughout his career, he argued that the Free Church was an institution committed to the doctrine of religious establishment. He quoted from a number references in an act of 1846 of the Free Church Assembly which stated:

> We firmly maintain the same scriptural principles as to the duties of nations and their rulers in reference to true religion and the Church of Christ, for which the Church of Scotland has hitherto contended.[60]

The advocates of the Voluntary position, and the forces within the Free Church willing to unite with the Voluntaries could change their minds in the light of such a testimony, or they could leave the Free Church to keep their conscience clear. What Begg was unwilling to allow them to do was to change the standards and testimony of the Free Church in order to fit their conscience and the views of the time. It is just at this point that Begg and Rainy differed so markedly. Rainy was willing to leave the standards

---

59. Ibid., p. 7.
60. Ibid., p. 9.

intact, but not to enforce the plain meaning of those standards. Begg would not have it. It was too much like a false testimony. No words were too strong for such actions, and Begg was willing to use strong words indeed:

> Suddenly a spirit of change seems to have seized on some of our leading men. The Church at large was not consulted or informed in regard to this, although this would only have been fair, as all were bound together by the most solemn mutual engagements. The people by whom the Church was upheld were not consulted. The representatives of those who had left large bequests to the Church were not consulted. No change was made in the solemn engagements undertaken in the sight of God by all our ministers and other office-bearers – viz., to abide by the original constitution. But in defiance of solemn vows and the brotherly covenant, Free Church principles were quietly being given up, and a determination was formed to carry the Church and her property, if possible, over to the United Presbyterians.[61]

It is here that Begg began to approach the great debate of Scottish Presbyterianism of the 19th and early 20th centuries regarding the legitimacy of changing constitutional standards of the Churches. Vows of ordination involve the individual with obligations of the most sacred character to the standards of the Church, to brother ministers who have also taken these vows, to the people who support a Church with such a standard, to the spirit of the fathers who established the testimony, and, in the case of the Established Church, an obligation to the Civil powers.

Whatever the specific votes, whatever the relative strength of the parties in the Church, Begg was certain that the testimony of

---

61. Ibid., p. 10.

the Free Church of Scotland, as set down in the documents of the constitutional standards, could not be altered without making an end to the Church itself.

> It is only after a generation has passed away that some leading men, who have apparently changed their own ground, and a number of young ministers who were not honoured to take part in the Disruption struggle, or to sacrifice anything for the principles of the Reformed Church of Scotland, are apparently seeking to shift the Free Church of Scotland from her original basis, and to identify her with the unscriptural and revolutionary principles of modern dissent. Fortunately, *the original documents remain and cannot be altered.*[62]

The other parties saw constitutional change, whether desirable or not in regard to any specific issue, as at least an option for the Church. But James Begg rejected any such suggestion. It was the unalterable constitution of the Free Church, including the principle of the Establishment of religion, which would save the denomination from the tyranny of the majority, in Begg's day or any other. Without such a provision, any group with sufficient support could change the face of the Free Church so as to make it unrecognizable to the founders. The Established Church had, at the very least, its relationship to the civil powers to keep it on the proper track. But the Free Church, without such a stay, needed the constitutional documents to reserve its testimony, its unique witness, its very being as an historical institution.

> Here, however, a very important and difficult question arises: How can Nonconformist Churches be kept to the maintenance of their own

---

62. Begg, *Memorial of Counsel*, p, 14.

principles? ... The constant appeals to "overwhelming majorities," in opposition to the principles of our Church, seem to prove that in the estimation of some even the fundamental principles of the Church may be subverted by mere numbers. The undoubted fact that we have a Constitution, which no power of numbers can alter, seems to be disregarded, if not denied, by some, and spiritual independence seems to be confounded with a right to do whatsoever we please.[63]

Of course, those who disagreed with Begg did have the votes in the Free Church General Assembly. What if the majority should decide to alter the standards of the Church in accordance with the opinions of the day? What would happen if the solemn vows were ignored and the impossible occurred? What of the faithful remnant and its testimony? The answer was given by James Begg in 1874, an answer which looked prophetically to the division of 1900 and the House of Lords' decision of 1904. The matter began with philosophical notions of vows and promises, and ended in questions of title to real property:

If our Church is to be altered without universal consent, all our arrangements must be commenced on a new footing, leaving the existing property to those who are still prepared and determined to stand on the old ground.[64]

Begg's Tactics

In his day, James Begg was accused of being a reactionary who clung stubbornly to the past in the face of all the progressive trends of the time. Yet, he was also recognized as an advocate

---

63. Ibid., p. 27.
64. Ibid., p. 26.

of social reform in regard to issues such as housing. This caricature obscures the fact that Begg used history and tradition as an instrument to do battle for those causes which he understood to be of significance for the contemporary and future godliness of the kingdom. Begg believed that he and his party were the true standard-bearers of the Scottish Reformed Church. It was his way of gaining support and legitimacy to claim to be one with the saints who had gone before.

Begg recognized that many did not share his view of the value of the traditional approach to Church and State relations; nevertheless he was optimistic, for he believed that his stand was for the truth and that the truth, which had brought glory to his nation and its Church in the past, would not be without its advocates in the future.

> A foolish and wicked anticipation has sometimes been expressed of late, that if a few men would only die out, the distinctive principles of the Disruption might be expected to be buried in their graves, but truth never dies any more than the God of truth, and when we see so many able and determined students adopting the true principles of the Disruption and ready to seize and bear aloft the old blue banner of Scotland's Church, when we are removed, we may "thank God and take courage," rejoicing in the certainty that a better day is about to dawn.[65]

Begg saw himself to be one with the Reformers, the Covenanters, the Fathers of the Disruption. The Unionists in the Free Church were attacking not merely Begg, but through him the worthies of Scotland's past.

---

65. Begg, *Principles, Position & Prospects*, p. 4.

It was of course the Disruption of 1843 which accounted for so much in the career of James Begg. He had been a part of that glorious day, he had been privileged to stand with Chalmers and the others for the cause of Christ. It was the great event of '43 which bound James Begg to those principles which otherwise might have been professed only as matters of debate or academic dispute. Begg did not merely believe in the principle of the establishment of religion, he had put his career on the line for it. It had become a sacred charge for him. He was not willing to allow the advocates of union to destroy the Free Church of Scotland. He defended the constitution of the Free Church because he believed in the importance of that Church's testimony. But his defense of the Free Church and the Disruption also must be understood as a result of the simple fact that he, James Begg, had been a part of the founding of that Church; he had participated in history in a visible fashion.

> What the principles of the Free Church are, in regard to the duty of nations towards the Church of Christ, as founded on the Word of God, is beyond all possibility of gainsaying. They are the hereditary principles of Scotland, and whatever others may do in regard to these principles, to them in their integrity we unalterably adhere. It was a dark day for our Church and country, as will yet be seen, when, in the fatal Assembly of 1867, it was resolved that these principles might be surrendered, or made "open questions," for the sake of an imaginary union. They are the only true principles of union; for the wisdom which cometh from above is *"first pure*, then peaceable," and there can be no true union of Christ's people which begins by denying the prerogatives of their glorious Head.[66]

---

66. James Begg, *Free Church Principles since the Disruption*. (Edinburgh: James Nichol, 1869), pp. 18-19.

Seeing himself as a defender of the principles of the Scottish Reformation and the Disruption, Begg was more than willing to draw the conclusion that those who opposed him were apostates from that tradition and traitors to that legacy. This was an approach used frequently by Begg in his speeches and writings during the Voluntary Controversy. The relative absence of biblical and theological analyses of the issues is offset by the abundance of material dealing with the question from the perspective of Scottish history and tradition.

It was Begg's concern for the principles of the Disruption which allowed him to oppose much that was being done in his day by the Church of the Disruption. His was anything but an unthinking allegiance to an institution. He was not concerned with maintaining the name of the Free Church at the expense of the standards of that Church. Begg was willing to leave the Free Church of Scotland when Free Church principles were no longer advocated by that Church. Begg lamented the decline of supporters for the principles of the Free Church and went on to assure his listeners that he, for one, was not willing to be a Free Churchman in name only.

> Do not deceive yourselves. I will not be a party to any such defection, and I will not come under such an obligation. I broke the fetters which bound me to the Established Church and I came out of one of the best of its manses and I never regretted it. I am bound to this Church only as long as this Church stands by the Truth – not one moment longer – and I will take my own way to apply that principle.[67]

Begg was prepared, if necessary, to leave the Free Church, but he was not willing to leave without a fight. His most extensive

---

67. Begg, *Present Aspect of the Union Question.*, p. 14.

work on the subject of the Establishment Principle and the union question was published in 1874 as *Memorial with the Opinions of Eminent Counsel in regard to the Constitution of the Free Church of Scotland and remarks on our present State and Prospects.* The work had been prepared for the General Assembly of 1872 when the possibility of a division in the Free Church was very real. It was understood to be a threat to the pro-Union party that the minority who supported the Establishment Principle was prepared to appeal to the civil courts should that Principle be disowned by the Assembly. The threat worked and the Church remained united, but the power of the appeal was not lost on any members of the Assemblies which followed. Its publication in 1874 showed that Begg was prepared to use such a legal appeal whenever it became necessary. Begg defined the basic purpose of the work as follows:

> The object of this publication is to demonstrate that the principle of National Religion is embedded in the Constitution of the Free Church of Scotland.[68]

Such a statement is incomplete, to say the least. This was not the whole of the purpose at all. The work was compiled not so much to state the principle as to threaten the opponents of that principle with serious consequences should it be disallowed by the Church. Later on in the book, Begg showed his real purpose by this statement:

> If our Church is to be altered without universal consent, all our arrangements must be commenced on a new footing, leaving the

---

68. Begg, *Memorial of Counsel.*, p. iii.

existing property to those who are still prepared and determined to stand on the old grounds.[69]

Here is the real thrust of the argument. It is not enough to see Begg as a defender of high principles alone. He was prepared to speak in the most material manner when necessary.

His opponents, then and now, have seen this appeal to the civil courts as a mark of Begg's evil genius, as evidence of his imperfect spirituality, as a clear indication of his false and unworthy motives. But such an evaluation of his tactics is unfair. One must understand this appeal to civil power and this concern with property as a means rather than an end. For Begg, such an appeal was the conclusion to a process, not the beginning. For one who believed in the national recognition of the Christian religion, in the Establishment of the Reformed Church in Scotland, an appeal such as this was the natural result. By this means, the seriousness of his purpose would be obvious to all and, at the same time, the whole question of the apostasy of his opponents would be laid bare.

Begg summarized the opinions of the learned counsel by noting the following four points:

> (1) that the Free Church has a Constitution which can be pleaded ... in a civil court; (2) that the Establishment principle is embodied in that Constitution, (3) that this cannot be made an open question; and (4) that no majority, however great, can alter this against the will of any minority, however small.[70]

---

69. Ibid., p. 16.
70. Ibid., p. 36.

Certainly, if the issue had gone as far as the civil courts in 1872, as it was to in 1900, this was the ground of the argument which Begg and his party would have presented.

It was while discussing these principles and tactics, that Begg dealt with the important issue of the contract between a non-established Church and the State. This was understood by him to be as serious a binding obligation as that of the minister's ordination vows. He was not prepared to be false to his conscience and his ordination engagements. In the same way and with the same degree of determination, he was not prepared to allow the Free Church, by whatever size majority, to be false to the contract established with the State in its constitution.

That the non-established Church had to recognize and deal with the State was, of course, obvious. But it shows the degree to which Voluntaryism had entered the thinking of many in the Free Church that Begg needed to remind the Church of this simple fact.

> It is not true that we are or can be entirely separated from the power of the State. The Church of Christ is *in* though not *of* the world. We do not refer to any special public advantages ... but we all have ecclesiastical property.[71]

Begg raised a question which was to be of considerable importance to the Church in Scotland throughout the rest of the century and into the present. It was a question which began with "the ecclesiastical property," but which went far beyond mere questions of title and ownership.

---

71. Ibid., p. 60.

Here, however, a very important and difficult question arises: How can Nonconformist Churches be kept to the maintenance of their own principles? ... The constant appeals to "overwhelming majorities," in opposition to the principles of our Church, seem to prove that in the estimation of some even the fundamental principles of the Church may be subverted by mere numbers.[72]

The State had a role to play in the Free Church of Scotland. It served as a court of appeal from any decision which subverted the fundamental constitution of that Church. Begg's question required a negative answer. No majority possessed the right to force a change in the Free Church which would make that institution something other than that originally founded in 1843. Its principles were not just outworn trappings from the past, of interest to antiquarians alone. Its principles were those ideals which gave substance and form to the Church's existence. The Free Church of Scotland was what it was not because of a name, or because of the possession of specific property, or because of the history of ecclesiastical succession, but because of the adherence of that Church to the principles set down at its foundation. Any change in these principles involved a fundamental change in the relationship between office-bearers and the Church. Begg firmly believed that to maintain these principles, to defend the existence of the Free Church as it was intended to be, an appeal to the civil courts was in order. A "contract" had been agreed to in 1843, and no majority in the General Assembly had any ecclesiastical or civil right to make that "contract" null and void.

---

72. Ibid., p. 28.

Begg recognized dangers in this concept of contract as the foundation for the State's dealings with non-established Churches, but there was a great opportunity as well. Any legal appeal required a definitive statement of the nature and substance of the Constitution of the Free Church. It was just this definitive, given nature which makes the documents of the Constitution so powerful in Begg's arsenal. The Free Church was founded, not upon some ill-defined, nebulous concept in the minds of the Disruption-Fathers, but upon documents, upon words written, printed, set down in black and white. What is the Constitution of the Free Church? Where is one to turn to find it? Not to the day-to-day actions of the Assembly, not to the opinions of the leading figures at one time of another, not to the political strength or weakness of a given party of faction, but to words written down for all to see. Begg defined the Constitution of the Free Church as including the following documents: The Claim of Right; the Protest; the Deed of Demission; the Formula. Begg continued:

> In reality, in conjunction with the Confession of Faith, they, and other standards to which the foresaid documents refer, form the Constitutions.[73]

This is the sort of thing that can be brought into civil courts. If the Constitution, as defined above, supports the doctrine of the Religious Establishment, then, Begg argued, the civil courts must find that to reject this doctrine was to make oneself something other than a Free Churchman. Begg suggested that he had had a

---

73. Ibid., p. 75.

vision of what such a decision would mean to the Scottish scene and the progress of the Unionist forces.

> This "contract" is entirely opposed to Voluntaryism: and if one or more members of a Free Church congregation were to demand from the civil court, on the ground of breach of contract, that their minister, having avowed Voluntary principles, should be found no longer entitled to live in his manse or to preach in his Church, we should like to know what would be the result?[74]

James Begg was willing to appeal to the civil courts if necessary to preserve the Establishment Principle in the Free Church of Scotland. He did so because the appeal itself was one of the principles he maintained, He was a son of the Disruption, one who had stood for the Free Church in 1843, but it was to the principles of that Church which he adhered, not to the name or structure alone. Such an appeal was a matter of great concern to the Unionist forces in 1872 and was the contributing factor in the moderation of their progress. It was all the more powerful a tactic because of its consistency with the whole of Begg's principles.

Issues Related to the Voluntary Controversy
The Establishment of the Church of Scotland

It has been suggested above that the first phase of the Voluntary Controversy led naturally to the second, namely, to the movement favoring the disestablishment of the Church of Scotland. As one who held to the principle of religious establishment, Begg opposed the movement. He presented the world with what might be considered a strange picture: the minister of a non-established Church

---

74. Ibid., p. 76.

doing battle with his fellow ministers in support of the establishment of the Church from which he had originally seceded. But the strangeness is not Begg's alone. The whole Disruption controversy fits into this picture, for the Free Church was leaving the Established Church while maintaining the Establishment Principle. It is significant that many within the Free Church were beginning to question the propriety of establishment, not merely in principle, but specifically in regard to the existing Church of Scotland. Many began to find affinity with the nonconformist churches in England, and looked more and more like dissenters from the idea of establishment as well as from the Established Church.

Begg responded to this agitation against establishment of the Church of Scotland by arguing that the principles of the Free Church required him to support the concept of establishment of religion, even though he could not in good conscience be a part of the Established Church itself. It was this system which had brought much good to Scotland and promised to be a most effective means of extending the influence of the Gospel in the future.

> The most thorough manifestation of National Religion consists not only in the recognition of Christianity in all our legislation and public acts, but in the maintenance of a Church Establishment, by which the knowledge of Divine truth, by means of a living ministry and the territorial [i.e. parochial; parish] system, may be diffused through every corner of the land.[75]

Begg recognized that should disestablishment occur, the results would be all the more serious because of the many ill effects

---

75. Begg, *Voluntaryism Indefensible*, p. 5.

which would accompany it. It was not merely a matter of the relationship between Church and State per se, but as has been shown above, the future happiness of Protestant Reformed Christianity in the United Kingdom was at stake.

Begg noted four specific dangers which he believed would accompany disestablishment.[76]

First of all, the Scottish nation would be throwing off its solemn obligations toward God Himself, by doing away with the public recognition of religion. Begg invoked the spirit of the Covenanters and pronounced the judgment of scripture on such an apostate land, "The nation and kingdom that will not serve thee shall perish, those nations shall be utterly wasted." (Isaiah 60:12).

Not only would covenants be broken and judgments laid down, but the future of non-Established Churches would be threatened also. Begg saw the solid Establishment of the Church of Scotland as a means of defense for Protestantism generally. Disestablishment was understood by Begg to be an overthrowing of the Revolution Settlement, and the whole structure of the body politic was therefore called into question. Certainly, the Protestantism of the Throne could no longer be assured. The Free Church might seek to rejoice over the fall of the Church of Scotland, but Begg argued that there could be no peace for the Free Church itself once the Protestant Establishment was destroyed.

Thirdly, Begg continued his line of reasoning by suggesting that as the Establishment went, so went the whole Christian fabric of society. The hope of truly evangelizing the land, a hope basic to the parish ideal, was now to be thrown away and nothing

---

76. Begg, *Principles, Position, and Prospects,* pp. 23-27

was to be put in its place but a continuation of the heathenism of Scotland.

Finally, disestablishment was surely an attempt to misuse property originally designated for the spiritual good of the nation. Endowments, manses, and churches would be put to other use, in spite of the needs of the people, and the ministers, so needed by the people, would be put out.

In all of this, Begg dealt with the grand theme of his view of the Establishment Principle, understood as a national confession of faith and a covenanting with the Lord God, but he also dealt with the mundane questions of property titles, endowments, and allocation of funds within the Church and State. Begg was not willing to treat the question only in the abstract. He saw the need for working out the practical implications of his principles. He moved over a wide range of issues all the way from the great themes of the Scottish Reformation to the immediate needs of his time, at once sweeping across the pages of history with a desire to present a vision of a truly biblical Reformed Church Establishment.

His opponents accused him of being desirous of the endowments and properties of the Church. But Begg recognized that there was an important distinction between the principle of establishment and the practice of State support.

> All who have ever intelligently maintained the Church Establishment principle have avowed this distinction, have held that endownments are not essential to a Church Establishment, in other words, are a consequence in proper circumstances of the Establishment principle, and not the principle itself. [77]

---

77. Begg, *Union Question*, p. 17.

Again, it must be stated that Begg's defense of the Establishment of the Church of Scotland was not primarily a concern for the financial control of glebes and tiends. These were a part of the Establishment in Scotland and could certainly be used in the cause of the Gospel, but this was not where Begg began. Rather, he was concerned with the Crown Rights of the Lord Jesus, with the cause of the national recognition of the Christian faith. He rejected any attempt to remove the outward evidence of this national recognition from the Scottish scene.

> It is a pure caricature and misrepresentation of our principles to say that we are looking to the Government for support, or that we reckon the support of the Government at all necessary in connexion with our maintenance as a Church. Our principle is, that the kings and governments of the earth are bound to acknowledge the supremacy of Christ, bound to acknowledge His Church, and, in proper circumstances, to endow that Church without enslaving it.[78]

The Establishment of the Church in Scotland was simply the practical working out of the biblical principle that nations as well as individuals were under the Judgment of Christ, who is Lord of all. The Church of Christ was required to labor in support of this principle, not because of a desire for lands and money, not for the personal gain of its ministers, but because of the demands of the Gospel itself.

> The real alternative placed before the country is that the Government shall become absolutely neutral, and assuredly you never are entitled on scriptural grounds to put that alternative to statesmen or to any

---

78. Ibid.

men ... All statesmen are bound to support the cause of Christ, and we must tell them so.[79]

The Establishment of the Church of Ireland

It was not in Scotland alone that the threat to Established Christianity was being raised in Begg's day. In Ireland the Established Church was episcopal in government and the move toward disestablishment made strange allies of the Roman Catholics and some Protestant non-conformists. Begg was not deceived by any such temporary alliance. Whatever the causes of the day, the only party which stood to gain should the Church of Ireland be disestablished was the Church of Rome.

> At the present moment parties are manifestly acting in concert whose objects are totally different, and never, perhaps, was the political craft of Rome more conspicuous than in getting so many opposite classes to do her work, and that too upon pretense of seeking to destroy her influence.[80]

Begg was concerned to show that the arguments of the anti-establishment forces in Ireland, Romanist and Protestant alike, were, in reality, serving the cause of Rome. Basically, the argument put forward for disestablishment was that the Episcopal Church of Ireland, Established by law, could not count on the support of the non-established Protestants, nor of the Roman Catholic majority in the kingdom. Protestant opponents argued that if one Church were to receive State support, then any and all Churches were entitled to this support. Thus, the continued Establishment of

---

79. Begg, *Proposed Disestablishment*, p. 7.
80. Ibid., p. 4.

the Church of Ireland, by this logic, required State support of Roman Catholic schools and churches, along with Presbyterians, Methodists, Baptists, etc. Since such support of Romanism was not acceptable to the Protestants, the only solution offered was to end all State support, to disestablish the Church of Ireland, to remain neutral in such affairs.

These were the alternatives put forward by the antiestablishment party in Ireland. James Begg was not willing to accept this analysis of the problem or the proposed solutions.

> We are no doubt bound to protest to the uttermost against indiscriminate endowments; and I, for my part, would go the length of saying that it is more impious to endow all than to endow none, and that the greatest calamity that could befall the country is the support of Popery by the Government in Ireland. But, on the other hand, I do not see – I have not been able to see – that the Government of this country, especially looking at it as the Government of the United Kingdom, a Protestant kingdom, of which Ireland is merely a part, are entitled to speak of having no alternative but to endow Popery, or to be neutral, or that we as a Christian Church, are entitled to tell them that any such alternative is presented to them.[81]

In spite of the opposition of some fellow non-conformists, Begg was willing to defend the Establishment in Ireland. It served as a bulwark against the increasing power of the Church of Rome, and kept the government of that land from giving in to the demands of those who advocated State neutrality which, as has been shown above, was only a mask for secularism, atheism, covenant-breaking. Thus, it was perfectly reasonable for James Begg, the minis-

---

81. Ibid., p. 9.

ter of the Free Church of Scotland, to support the Establishment of the Church of Ireland. Indeed, such support had the warrant of Knox and Chalmers. It was a fallacy to argue to the contrary, that only complete agreement in government and doctrine could allow for the support of a given Establishment.[82]

The Aftermath of the Conflict

James Begg died in 1883, but the issues which he raised in the Voluntary Controversy did not die with him.[83] The Free Church of Scotland was to be a Church divided by party spirit for the rest of the century. As Begg had prophesied, the pro-Unionists waited until the vocal leaders who opposed them were dead to bring up the question of Union with the United Presbyterian Church. By the close of the 1880's an attempt was being made to pass a Declaratory Act in the General Assembly of the Free Church. This Act dealt with a number of theological points which seemed on the face of it merely matters needing greater clarification. But there were two dangers in the Act from the point of view of the Constitutional Party. First, the Act went beyond the Confession of Faith and laid down as principles of the Free Church that which was not explicitly taught in the Confession. (For example, the salvation of *all* who die in infancy is affirmed.) Secondly, the Act was recognized as a means by which ordination ties to all the teachings of the Confession might be overcome. The Act declared:

---

82. James Begg, *The Late Dr Chalmers on the Establishment Principle and Irish Protestantism* ... (Edinburgh: James Nichol, 1568), p. 23. See also pp. 24-32.

83. See the standard works on the period, Burleigh, Fleming, Collins and the *History of the F.P. Church*.

that, while diversity of opinion is recognized in this Church on such points in the Confession as do not enter into the substance of the Reformed Faith therein set forth, the Church retains full authority to determine, in any case which may arise, what points fall within this description, and thus to guard against any abuse of this liberty to the detriment of sound doctrine, or to the injury of her unity and peace.[84]

The Church itself, that is the majority of any meeting of the General Assembly, thus received the power to determine what was or was not binding in the Confession. This was directly opposed to the thought of the Constitutional Party which argued that the Confession itself, the words of the document, were to be the final judge of binding doctrine. By means of the Declaratory Act, any theological principle, even though clearly taught by the Confession, might be declared to be outside the "substance of the Reformed Faith" and thereby those who would not affirm such a doctrine might be received into or remain in the ministry of the Free Church.

The Act had been approved by the General Assembly and sent down to the Presbyteries under the terms of the Barrier Act of 1697. When the Assembly met again in 1892, it was learned that a majority of the Presbyteries had approved the Act. It thus became the law of the Church. Many in the Free Church seemed ready to leave the denomination. Meetings were held where ministers, elders, and divinity students expressed theirs fears. An attempt was to be made to repeal the Act at the Assembly of 1893. Such an attempt failed, but the actual number of ministers who proved willing to leave the Church was small indeed. The manner of men

---

84. *History of the Free Presbyterian Church*, p. 61.

who had fought in Begg's day were noted by their absence in the 1893 Assembly. Only Donald Macfarlane stood against the Act by tabling a Protest and leaving the Assembly. Later to be joined by Donald MacDonald, and other elders and students, he formed what was to become the Free Presbyterian Church of Scotland. It claimed to be the Church of the Disruption and made much of the principles of James Begg.

With the Declaratory Act passed by the Free Church, the move toward Union with the United Presbyterians was now open. A Committee was organized for this purpose in 1897, and by 1900 all was ready. A last attempt was made to oppose the Union by a minority of the 1900 Assembly, but it was approved by the Church. The minority, locked out of the Free Church College and Assembly Hall, moved to a rented hall and continued the work and witness of the Free Church of Scotland. The legal appeal threatened by James Begg in 1872 now became a reality. The appeal was taken to the Law Lords and a decision given in 1904 in favor of the minority. Begg's principles had won the day.

Although he did not live to see it, the events of 1893 and 1900-1904 vindicated Begg as a prophet, if not as a politician. He had argued that a fundamental change in the Constitution of the Free Church would require the loyal minority to leave for the sake of conscience. Such a change took place in 1893 and a minority, although small, left the Church. Begg argued in his *Memorial of Counsel* that the law of the land had to recognize a faithful minority as the spiritual and temporal successor to the Free Church. Such a minority continued in 1900 and the House of Lords itself recognized its claim. Begg did not win all of the great battles of his day, but his principles in regard to the questions of the Constitution of the Free Church of Scotland have been proved true by the facts of history.

Chapter II

SOCIAL PROBLEMS AND THEIR REFORM

Housing for the Working Class

JAMES Begg was a man with a vision of what the Christian Gospel might bring to Scotland, if applied to the social problems of his day. It was to require no small effort on his part to define these problems, bring them to the attention of Church and State, suggest practical solutions, and, all the while, keep the Gospel at the forefront of the struggle.

The housing problem had been recognized by many as a serious one. A number of accounts of the extreme poverty, want of basic necessities, and general filth [squalor] which constituted much of Scotland's housing had been brought before the public in the 1840's.[1] The remarks of William Chambers serve as an illustration of these analyses:

> ... in spite of the vigorous regulations to the contrary, the closes which are inhabited by the poorer classes continue in a most filthy condition both night and day ... I feel convinced that there is as

---

1. Stewart Mechie, *The Church and Scottish Social Development 1780-1870*. (London: Oxford University Press, 1960), pp. 122-123.

great a moral evil ... Society, in the densely peopled closes which I have alluded to, has sunk to something indescribably vile and abject. Human beings are living in a state worse than brutes. They have gravitated to a point of wretchedness from which no effort of the pulpit, the press or the schoolmaster can raise them.[2]

Begg's concern was not with the immediate problem of housing alone. In a sense the whole matter of social unrest in the nineteenth century was understood by Begg to be a result of poor housing. But poor housing would not be solved by merely improving the quality of the buildings; instead financial, legal and social changes were required which would foster rather than discourage individual private ownership of houses.

An examination of the state of housing in Scotland was a means by which the social health of the community might be determined.

We hold it to be a clear dictate of reason and experience, that a nation's social *state* is proved, and that men's moral and social condition may be more certainly determined by an examination of the dwellings of the masses of the people, than by any other external test.[3]

If this was true, then the social state of Scotland was poor indeed. The 1861 census revealed the following shocking facts:

Of 666,786 houses in Scotland there were 7,964 without windows, and 225,723 houses of one apartment, which meant that about one million people, or nearly one-third of the entire population, were living in one-apartment houses. Not only so, but of these one-roomed

---

2. Ibid., p. 122.

3. James Begg, *Happy Homes for Working Men, and How to Get Them.* (London: Cassell, Petter, & Galpin; Edinburgh: James Nichol, 1866), p. 13.

houses 40,703 had each from 6 to 16 human beings residing in them. In Edinburgh there were 121 single-roomed houses without a window; there were 13,209 families, representing at least 50,000 of the population, living in houses of only one apartment, and of these one-roomed houses 1,530 had each from 6 to 15 inhabitants. In Glasgow there were 241 one-roomed houses without a window; and 28,269 houses with only one apartment each, containing a population of at least 100,000; and of these one-roomed houses 2,212 had each from 7 to 15 inhabitants.[4]

The causes of this immense problem were not technical; it was certainly possible to build more adequate housing. Rather, the problems were a result of the very nature of Scottish society. Begg singled out the peculiarities of the Reformation settlement for blame here. The land formerly held by the Roman Church had been distributed to a select few of the nobility and their descendants still held it. Coupled with antiquated legal bars to selling much of the land and property, the kingdom of Scotland found itself by the nineteenth century to be unique among the nations of Europe, in that its land was held by fewer individuals than any other country.[5] Begg set himself a task which would require him to fight against much that was entrenched in the traditions of his country. It is clear that his view of the Gospel and its social implications required him to do nothing less.

Concern with the housing problem grew in Scotland in the 1840's. The first attempt to build better housing for the working classes was begun in 1851. Begg traveled throughout the United

---

4. Mechie. p. 129.

5. Begg, *Happy Homes*, p. v.

Kingdom to study the plans and gain the support of others who were interested in the housing questions. In 1855-1858 Begg sponsored the visits to Scotland of James Taylor of Birmingham, a leader in this movement for reform. In 1858, Begg convinced the Free Church General Assembly to take the matter seriously and a Committee was appointed with Begg serving as Convener. Each year a report was submitted by this Committee to the Assembly detailing the problems and suggesting solutions. Attempts were made to mobilize the Free Church for concerted work in this area. The statistics of the census report for 1861 were reported to the Assembly and Begg was able to rejoice that "The idea that Christian men and ministers have no interest in the question is almost entirely dispelled." [6] The Assembly went so far as to request the Government to appoint a Royal Commission to study the housing problem in Scotland. Begg himself was involved in the work of the Edinburgh Co-operative Building Society and other groups and financial institutions, having the honor of laying the foundation stone of the Company's first row of houses in October 1861. Begg continued to work with his Church and with private bodies to achieve his goals, as well as to petition the Government when necessary. [7]

Writing in 1866, Begg gave the following account of his concern with the housing question:

The attention of the author was directed to this subject more than twenty-five years ago, both by a personal inspection of the most degraded districts of Glasgow and Edinburgh, and by his observa-

---

6. Mechie, pp. 127-128.

7. See Begg, *Happy Homes*, pp. 15-34, and Mechie, pp. 126-130.

tions as a minister of a country parish. From that period till the present he has never ceased in every competent way to call attention to its importance. At the first period referred to, the matter excited little or no interest in the general community; and even when it did afterwards begin to engage attention, schemes of remedy were suggested which were totally inadequate to meet the case ... but we have been privileged to see the dawn of a brighter day; and in the history which I am about to give of the operations and success of the Co-operative Building Society of Edinburgh we see a demonstration that the whole problem, great as it is, may, by the Divine blessing, be entirely solved by the resources and power of the people themselves, if only properly combined; whilst it can be solved in no other way.[8]

Begg's writings on the housing problem reveal four principles which served as a foundation for his labors in this regard.

First, Begg saw the goal of "every man his own landlord" as one worthy of support in its own right, but also as the source of much good for other social and moral interests. The ideal of an individually owned home was one which was of interest to the Christian minister and social reformer alike. Begg described the principle in this way:

... that the family system, like the Sabbath Law, being an institution of Paradise, is essentially connected with the permanent wellbeing of man. No mere extension of barrack accommodation will therefore cure the evil which exists. Man must not only have a covering, but a *Home*. God made men in families; and it is upon the right maintenance and ordering of these little kingdoms that the peace and social order of all the great kingdoms of the world depends ... the experi-

---

8. Begg, *Happy Homes*, pp. 14-15.

ence of all ages proves, moreover, that to destroy this is to dissolve society; whilst to have this home duly established, and our own, and therefore to have an absolute control over it – to have its arrangements adapted alike to physical comfort and Christian progress, – is an essential condition of individual happiness, Christian security, and national wellbeing, as well as a hopeful precursor of eternal joy.[9]

It was this goal, a family living in its own dwelling, which was the great aim of Begg's labors for social reform. It was much more than a search for mere physical comfort. It was a search for a solid foundation for society, a society which Begg believed ought to be a just, orderly, Christian one. Nothing less than the prosperity, physical, social, spiritual, was at stake.

Begg pressed toward this goal not just as a reformer concerned with the prosperity of the land, but as a Christian. Social improvement and national prosperity were important to James Begg, but his concern was always beyond this to the vision of the Gospel applied to family living. It was not just a matter of stone and mortar, of investments and mortgages; it had to be one of faith and prayer as well.

It would be a still greater misinterpretation of our drift and design in this struggle to suppose that we anticipated any great ultimate result and especially the regeneration of human society, from the mere multiplication of comfortable dwellings, apart from the fear and grace of God. It is a vast step in advance no doubt, to secure such dwellings ... but the multiplication of Bethels, – houses in which the fear and worship of God shall be found, – is what we really want.[10]

---

9. Begg, *Happy Homes*, p. lv.

10. Ibid., p. 63.

The second principle underlying Begg's work was that the working class itself must be involved in the task of achieving this goal. Begg was unwilling to subject these men to charity. Houses would not be provided for them; rather they would organize themselves in such a way that it might be said that they built and paid for their own housing. This appears to have been in contrast to the practice of others workers in this area of housing reform. Begg sounds quite modern in his defense of the self-respect of those for whom he sought to labor. "The notion of treating working men as a kind of grown children, for whom everything must be provided is repugnant to their own better feelings ... " [11]

Begg wanted the working class itself to be involved in the task of providing new housing because he recognized that their longing for better living conditions was a desire which could be of great help to the cause. That such men possessed this desire was a matter for thanksgiving. Begg argued that it ought to be cultivated and supported by Church and State alike.

> You will not find in Scripture, therefore, any countenance given to the idea that it is not the duty of men, and even of Christians, earnestly to study, although, of course, in a subordinate view to promote their independence, in so far as men are concerned, even in the present world.[12]

A third principle can be defined as Christian motivation for social reform. Begg did not see his labor in this area as a secondary interest over and apart from his role as a Christian minister. His calling as a Free Church minister was one which included involve-

---

11. Ibid., p. 17.
12. Ibid., p. 109.

ment in the social problems of his people. His vision of the Free Church as an instrument of God for bringing the Gospel to the whole of Scotland included a definite place for such social reform.

As early as 1849, Begg expressed concern for the role of the Free Church in the poorer districts of the major cities of Scotland. He was to be a vocal defender of principle that the Church had a role to play in social reform. For Begg, this was not something new, recently discovered in the nineteenth century, but was a part of the Reformed tradition in Scotland. The Church's role in social and political affairs had a long history.

> Whilst I cordially say that everything pertaining to the mere partisan of political ought always to be banished from the courts of this Church, the social condition and the physical circumstances of the people are matters with which we have much to do ... I see these men [Knox and others] great as ministers of Christ, and at the same time prominent in promoting every object by which the temporal prosperity of the people may be advanced.[13]

Begg pointed to the Shorter Catechism's answer regarding the eighth commandment as clear evidence that a Christian must be concerned with "the lawful procuring and furthering the wealth and outward estate of ourselves and others."[14]

Begg took pains to remind his listeners time and again of the connection between the Christian Gospel and social reforms. He did this because he believed that the Gospel required such involvement and also because only in the Gospel was a true and lasting solution to society's problems to be found. Both the

---

13. Mechie, pp. 119-120.
14. Ibid., p. 120.

Churchman and the Reformer needed to have the point stressed. The example of Christ himself was invoked to show that proper housing was of concern to Christians.

> Our blessed Lord supposes the existence, not only of a home, but of a house with more apartments than one, and even of a feeling of independence, when He says, "Enter into *thy* closet, and shut the door ..."[15]

Clearly, a large number of the inhabitants of Glasgow and Edinburgh could not follow the Lord's command in this regard and it was necessary for Christ's Church through members and officers alike to speak out and take action.

Begg was aware that good and proper housing was not the only need of the people, and certainly recognized that the Church's concern for them could not cease when housing had been provided. But he was willing to assert that whatever might follow, the provision of proper housing, as difficult as that goal might be to attain, must rank first in the area of social reforms.

> ... whilst the grand cure for the woes of society is only to be found in the gospel of the grace of God, and in that new heart and right spirit without which man must in any circumstances remain depraved and miserable, the most important physical remedy for the woes of man is a comfortable and wholesome dwelling.[16]

The fourth principle which can be seen to underlie Begg's work of social reform is one which was not specifically articulated by him very often, but which does appear as a presupposition for much of

---

15. Begg, *Happy Homes*, pp. 63-64.
16. Ibid., p.9.

his work and writings. That is the responsibility of society at large for the poor among it. Begg believed that such a responsibility was a serious one. Individuals as Christians and as citizens were required to be involved in such work. The Government itself faced a similar responsibility. Of course, there were those who argued to the contrary, and defended their lack of action by pleading their rights as individuals. Begg would not accept such an argument. He was certainly not one with the Socialists, but he was not willing to allow such talk to hide the Christian's duty in matters of social reform.

> The supreme rule of legislation ought to be, the framing of all measures to promote the wellbeing of society at large, and that to this object all individual rights, real or imaginary, are subordinate.[17]

These principles were articulated in Begg's major published work on the housing question, *Happy Homes for Working Men and How to Get Them*, brought out in 1866. As always, Begg was a practical man. Theories and principles were fine, but they were not enough in themselves. One must provide a serious scheme for achieving the desired reforms, spelled out in detail, with objections answered, if the goal of such principles was ever to see the light of day. Such was the purpose of *Happy Homes* … :

> The object of the present work is strictly practical. The existence of an enormous evil, destructive alike to comfort, health, life, and morality, is assumed – a great social gangrene, eating out the very vitals of society … the only real question which now remains is, How is this great evil to be remedied?[18]

---

17. Ibid., p. 55.
18. Ibid., p. iii-iv.

Begg hoped that his book would be used by reformers like himself, but also by the workingmen whose need of proper housing was so great. The workings of the Edinburgh Co-operative Building Society were spelled out in detail, charts and tables showed how finances were to be organized, illustrations were provided of the Society's projects in Edinburgh so that others might be inspired to do likewise. The purpose of the publication was not theoretical at all; instead it was to be a manual dealing with the immediate practical questions, and all the while, a tract designed to inspire and encourage others engaged in the struggle.

> The book, as a whole, may therefore, it is hoped, by the blessing of God, furnish a kind of manual or *handbook* on probably by far the most important social question of the day.[19]

The problem of the day was the lack of suitable housing in the cities of Scotland. The practical solution suggested by Begg consisted of two steps.

> ... the first step necessary is to bring suitable houses into existence in sufficient numbers ...[20]

This step necessitated the acquisition of property, the planning and execution of the construction, the various legal requirements throughout the process and, finally, the sale of the completed dwellings to working families. But such construction was not sufficient in itself if the sales could not be made. The workingmen needed funds in order to purchase the dwellings. Begg suggested

---

19. Ibid., p. vi.
20. Ibid., p. iv.

a second step which would enable the working class to achieve the great goal of owning their own homes.

> The second and equally important step in the process, but making the process complete, is the acquiring of such houses on the principle of periodical payments terminating in a limited number of years, and leaving the owner in absolute possession of his own house.[21]

This was a proposal for the now commonly accepted process of amortizing mortgages over a fixed term with a constant payment. This enabled many to contemplate the ownership of a house, who would never have been able to do so if they were required to wait until such a large sum of money had been made available from their savings. Begg showed that such a scheme was a practical means of achieving his goal, and offered the example of the Joint-Stock Building Societies as an institution which would enable his two-fold solution to become a reality.

Of course, there were problems facing the advocates of such a housing scheme. Begg suggested three serious difficulties standing in the way of his project:

> I. The comparative want of sympathy with this movement, on the part of some of the higher classes of society in Scotland ... II. The second obstacle in the way of the progress of this movement is connected with the difficulty and expense of titles in Scotland to heritable property ... III. The greatest of all the difficulties remains, viz., the difficulty in the acquisition of land upon which the houses may be erected.[22]

---

21. Ibid., p. v.
22. Ibid., pp. 48-54.

With these difficulties in mind, Begg detailed a number of ways of moving toward the goal. In a sense, of course, the whole of his lecturing and publishing work was an attempt to enlist the support of the "higher classes" in the venture. The enthusiastic support given to the housing reform proposals by the General Assembly of the Free Church, in response to the Committee reports of James Begg, was a definite step in this direction.

Apart from this general appeal to the nation, Begg labored specifically for the Edinburgh Building Society. He detailed plans for "continually turned over capital" which would be used to finance housing projects in the city, with the understanding that payments made by the new working class owners would be put back into new construction, thereby providing, according to Begg, "an indefinite number of houses." [23]

The legal difficulties were more serious. Two problems were involved. The first was the basic feudal principle, enshrined in Scots Law in a number of ways, which made it difficult for many landowners to sell their property. Begg, like other reformers, spoke out strongly against these legal impediments to social progress:

> It is quite plain that the old feudal system is tottering to decay, and that a large portion of these lands is only held by the proprietors because they are bound to them by the stringent, but, I hold, the most unchristian fetters of the law of entail ... Let the law of entail be abolished. The sooner the entail system is extirpated the better. [24]

---

23. Ibid., p. 25,
24. Ibid., p. 131.

But even this was not enough. The process of transferring title to heritable property in Scotland was involved and the possibility for error was great. Many landowners were unsure of the strength of their titles. Though some lawyers found such confusion profitable, many were offering suggestions for legal reform based on the model of English law. Begg supported this move for reform and offered suggestions in *Happy Homes* ... for the working out of such a welcome change in the law.

In considering these plans of James Begg, one must keep in mind at all times the ardent concern which he showed for the people for whom he labored. As has been mentioned above, Begg wished for the working men themselves to be involved in the housing plans and active in the Building societies. Begg could never be the cold, impersonal reformer. His interest in the lives of the people was sincere and encompassed all of his projects on their behalf. Others might suggest grand plans for re-development of the cities, but Begg knew that all such plans must take into consideration the practical effect upon the individuals involved in them. He was particularly concerned to oppose mass displacement of people, a state of affairs which was all too common in his day, particularly as a result of the building of the railroads in urban areas. The human problem could not be ignored, even when such plans were admirable in themselves.

A very natural idea, no doubt, is that new streets should be driven *at once* through the dense centres of our cities, as a means of curing the evil. If our excellent friends would reflect for a moment, they must see that, until new houses are provided for the people, the making of such streets would in the first place only augment the existing evils. For what is to become of the wretched inhabitants thus dis-

70

lodged in the meantime? They cannot be turned into the street; and the effect of ploughing through their wretched dwellings, and thus setting them adrift, *in the first instance,* is only to make them crowd more fearfully the miserable houses which remain, and thus make them more pestilential.[25]

Begg argued that the results of housing schemes such as those begun in Edinburgh would be of benefit to the whole of Scottish society. The first beneficial result would be the obvious one; in the place of wretched, rented quarters, working men would now be living in well-equipped, solidly built homes which they them-selves owned and cared for. They would do so not as a result of charity from some great benefactor, but because of their own sense of purpose, organization, and financial sacrifice. This in itself would be an admirable result from both a humanitarian and a Christian perspective.

A second benefit would accompany the first. Society would find itself more ordered and prosperous. The potential disor-ders of a large population of working poor, miserably housed, open to social revolution and riot, would be replaced with the ordered reliability of those who shared with the rich in a por-tion of the land of Scotland. They would be their own landlords, indeed.[26]

Finally, Begg saw a great benefit in such housing plans as they might be applied to the Highlands and Islands of Scotland. Suggesting such a plan for the Isle of Islay, Begg argued that to sell lots at £200 each on the island would provide an opportunity

25. Ibid., p. 21.
26. Ibid., pp. 113-114.

for those who had thought of leaving Scotland altogether to settle instead a few hours' sail from Glasgow.

> And then, look at the advantages to the country. Who are the men that are driven out of the country by means of this forced emigration? they are the very backbone and sinew of the country.[27]

A loss such as this, a loss to Scotland, to the Free Church, possibly even to Christianity itself, could be averted by plans for housing such as those of James Begg.

Begg had a vision of what Scotland could be. It was to be a land where the Gospel was not only accepted in principle but applied in practice, a land where men were able to train their children in the things of Christ by daily worship in a sound, safe comfortable home which was their own. Such a vision has rightly been described as "a property-owning Christian democracy."[28] Begg would have accepted that description of his goal, but he would have gone on to argue that all three parts of the description were essential to the success of the whole.

The Seat Rent Question

James Begg's concern for social reform was not limited to the housing problem. He wrote three works on the subject of seat rents, one of which was eighty-eight pages in length. Such an issue may seem relatively unimportant for modern Christians, but the question was one of significance to a man such as Begg who sought to apply the Christian Gospel to the whole of life. Indeed,

---

27. Ibid a, p. 133.

28. James Begg, *Seat Rents brought to the Test of Scripture, Law, Reason and Experience* ... (Edinburgh: John Johnstone, 1838), p. v.

he argued, the seat rent question, "lies at the very foundation of many controversies of the present day, and of the success of the Assembly's Church Extension Scheme."[29] The scheme in question was that of the Established Church, for this book was written in 1838 prior to the Disruption. Begg recognized that in dealing with the seat rent question he was dealing with an issue which had to be resolved in a biblical way if the desire of the Church to minister to all of society was to be achieved.

The problem was that if rents were to be charged for seats in the Church, what was to be the status of those who could not pay? Obviously, these people had two options, they could simply absent themselves from the Churches or they could accept the free seating provided for the poor. Both of these were abhorrent to James Begg.

If the poor stayed away from the Church of Jesus Christ because they could not afford to attend, then something was very wrong with the witness of that Church. And yet, as he analyzes the situation in Scotland, such was indeed the case.

> It is a most striking fact, not only that there are in Edinburgh nearly 50,000 persons, and in Glasgow 65,000, who never attend public worship, but that these are *all of the poorer classes chiefly of the very lowest*. Now, in the country parishes, the very poorest, the very beggars, are found in the House of God, and are sometimes most regular attenders. As common people heard the Gospel of old gladly, so do they still, where there are no seat rents.[30]

Those who approved of seat rents argued that provision had been made for the poor by the practice of offering them free seating.

---

29. Ibid.
30. Ibid., p. 67.

Begg was always concerned with the self-respect of those for whom he labored in his social reform work, and therefore such a suggestion was not at all acceptable to him. He knew the strength of public opinion, of gossip, of evil talk. He knew, too, the need for self-esteem, the need to maintain oneself free from charity and the whims of one's betters.

> Now the whole of this misunderstanding arises from confounding *free* sittings with *pauper* sittings. To receive seats for nothing *because we are poor*, when all the rest of the congregation are paying for them, and thus to have our poverty branded with a stigma before our neighbours, is certainly what no one likes: but for rich and poor to meet together on the same terms, and enjoy the Gospel without money, as the inhabitants of a mountain glen equally enjoy the free and pure stream of their native hills, is undoubtedly a blessing which can only be undervalued by those who know not and have never experienced what it is.[31]

Even this was not the end of the dangers inherent in the seat rent system. Christian charity and the joy of giving to the Lord's work was entirely absent when funds for the Church were raised in the form of taxes on seating. Even the rich man, who could afford such a seat, suffered from the system which did not allow Christian giving to take the form it should.

> Our anxious desire is to set the people individually entirely free from payment and obligations of every kind, except in so far as the love of Christ shall constrain them freely to give for the advancement of his cause.[32]

---

31. Ibid., pp. v-vi.
32. Ibid., p. viii.

The goal for James Begg as he wrote in 1838 from within the Established Church was the entire elimination of seat rents from the Scottish scene.[33] As a Free Church minister in 1843, his task was to prevent such an evil from being introduced into the newly formed Church.

The basic question put by James Begg was this:

> Does Scripture ... give us any principle, warranting the imposition of a tax upon the public worship of God, like that which we call seat rents?[34]

The testimony of the Scriptures was, of course, the basic consideration, whatever the dictates of reason or experience. Begg argued that reason and experience also were opposed to such a practice, but it was from the scriptural argument that he drew his greatest strength. It was not just a matter of pragmatic concern for the immediate situation, but a great and general teaching of the Scriptures, at the heart of the Christian faith, was at stake.

> Therefore, to put a tax on the public worship of God – to make the payment of money as an essential prerequisite to hearing the Gospel must clearly frustrate the design of Christ; for men, instead of over-leaping such a barrier will rather say to God, "Depart from us, we desire not the knowledge of thy ways."[35]

Begg advanced three principles from the Bible which were opposed to the practice of seat rents. This shows Begg's concern to operate as a biblical Christian, as one who took seriously the whole counsel of God and applied it to all of his life and work.

---

33. Ibid., p. 11.
34. Ibid., p.13.
35. Ibid., p. 13.

The first principle relating to the seat rent question was:

> ... that the proclamation of the Gospel was intended to be quite free – as free as the circulation of the air of heaven, as free as the water which flows from the everlasting hills.[36]

In support of this principle, Begg quotes extensively from the Bible, including such passages as Psalm 68:10; Isaiah 55:1; Matthew 11:5; 28:19,30; Luke 14:12; and Revelation 22:17. In regard to the last text mentioned, "And whosoever will, let him take the water of life freely," Begg asks:

> ... whether it is possible to write this inscription over any church groaning under the burden of oppressive seat rents? Something more than will is required now, to procure admission into the places where the mysteries of Christ are dispersed. There must be the golden or silver key to open the door.[37]

Begg discovered a second principle relevant to the discussion in the example of the apostles themselves. He argued that they fulfilled the command of Christ literally by preaching to the people "without money and without price." If such was the example of the apostles, then the modern Church of Christ can do no less; therefore, barriers by way of fees and rents have no place in the Church.[38]

Thirdly, not only does the Bible encourage such a free offer of the Gospel, it positively condemns any mercenary motive in the work of the Church. He quotes in this regard from John. 2:16

---

36. Ibid., p. 14.
37. Ibid., p. 18.
38. Ibid.

and, with special emphasis, James 2:1-4. Begg saw this passage as one of great importance in the discussion of seat rents, for, to his mind, the seat rent system is directly condemned by the Apostle. James condemns those who "have respect to him that weareth the gay clothing, and say unto him, Sit thou here in a good place; and say to the poor, Stand thou there, or sit here under my footstool" (James 2:4). Begg concluded from this passage:

> Now, I wish you to observe, that what is here so unsparingly condemned is not nearly so bad as what I have experienced myself of old, in one of the churches of Edinburgh. James does not speak of any surly doorkeepers, standing to prevent the poor from entering the church at all ... He does not intimate that a time would ever come in the history of the Christian Church when the poor would actually be kept out of the House of God altogether, and made to hurry back into deeper obscurity, – perhaps plunge into deeper vice than before.[39]

When dealing with the housing problem, Begg was not content merely to lament the poor state of housing in the cities, he went on to engage himself in practical programs to remove the evil. So, too, in regard to seat rents, Begg suggested that the financing of the Church could be more profitably achieved by means other than seat rents, and he encouraged those who shared his views to work in the political arena to achieve their goals.

In answering his own question, "What ought those opposed to seat rents do?" Begg suggested four steps which might be taken:

> 1. If they pay the seat rents demanded by the Magistrates, let it be under protest ... 2. Let them give liberally towards carrying forward

---

39. Ibid., p. 23.

the present process [a move to have seat rents declared illegal] …
3. Let them send to the Town-Council only such men as are sound
in their views of the seat rent question. 4. Let them zealously spread
information abroad on the principles and facts of this important
controversy.[40]

Here we see Begg in a typical stance. Protesting against injustice, working and giving to the cause, using all the legal means of
redress, and publicizing the issue throughout the land.

Most of the material quoted above was written before the
Disruption. In 1843, Begg published a pamphlet opposing any
move toward the introduction of seat rents in the Free Church.
Here the issue was not one which required action in Town
Councils and Civil Courts, but argument in the Presbyteries and
Assemblies of the Free Church itself.

Begg assured his readers that his opposition to seat rents in
the Free Church did not mean that the worshippers were to be
exempt from payment toward the support of the Church. The
issue was not the propriety of congregational support for the
Church and the ministry. Rather, the debate was over the means
by which such giving was to be fostered. Secondly, Begg was not
opposed to the allocation of seats in the Church. Assignments
to specific seats fostered reverent behavior in the house of God
and were in no sense condemned by the Word. Payment for
such seats was the great evil.[41]

---

40. James Begg, *The Seat-Rent Question* (Edinburgh: John Johnstone, 1839),
pp. 15-16.

41. James Begg, *Reasons Why No Seat-Rents should be in the Free Church*
(Edinburgh: John Johnstone, 1843), pp. 1-2.

Begg's argument against seat rents and their introduction in the Free Church was based on five principles which he summarized as follows:

> (1) Seat-rents present an undoubted barrier to the free preaching of the gospel ... (2) Seat-rents shift the responsibility of determining *how much* a man is to give to the cause of Christ from a man's own conscience, where God has placed it, and makes it rest in a great measure with the managers of a congregation ... (3) Does not this system of letting the house of God tend to bring human passions into the Church, and to graft the suspicion of the world of merchandise on the free spirit of Christianity? ... (4) Seat-rents in a crowded church, undoubtedly arrest the stream of benevolence ... (5) But, in our estimation, the crowning practical objection to this system is, that it always bears down heavily and oppressively on the poor and working classes.[42]

Conclusion to Chapter II

As has been shown above, James Begg was vitally concerned with issues of social reform in his day. He did so not as something extra, outside of his task as a minister of the Gospel, but as one who saw that calling to be inclusive of such social actions. The report to the Free Church General Assembly of 1862 by the Committee on housing chaired by Begg summarized his views on the role of the Church in matters of social reform.

> ... a spiritual canker has invaded many in all parts of the Protestant Church – not only the idea that the ministers of Christ have nothing to do with such so-called secular matters as the houses of the people, but that to manifest an utter indifference upon the whole subject is

---

42. Ibid., pp.2-3.

a mark of superior sanctity. To our mind this is not simply a reversal of the whole spirit of the Bible and the Reformation, it is a "glorying in our shame." [43]

Begg was a minister who expended great energy in the cause of social reform. The issues of housing and seat rents have been examined above, for these were the issues which resulted in substantial published work. But he was also involved in debates on education, the extension of the franchise, the shorter work day, the maintenance of the Sabbath, and the provision of public parks and gardens in the cities. His social conscience extended beyond the borders of Scotland and the United Kingdom and he was involved in opposition to the opium trade.

As he was unwilling to allow the State to ignore its responsibility to the Church, so too he was determined to take seriously the civil and social implications of the Good News which the Church was called to preach.

---

43. Mechie, p. 128.

Chapter III

THE ROMANIST THREAT

IN chapter I of this paper, much was made of the importance of the Roman Church in Begg's stand for the Establishment Principle. He argued that it was as a firm bulwark against Romanism that the Establishments deserved the support of Christians in England, Scotland, and Ireland. It was the Church of Rome which stood to gain should the Protestant Establishments be removed in the United Kingdom. Its aggression would be seen not only in the strictly ecclesiastical matters but in the whole of life in the nation, politically, intellectually, culturally. Begg waged a life-long battle against the Roman Church and sought to call the attention of other Christians to the great danger and of the need for serious confrontation with what he believed to be the power of the biblical Antichrist.

No doubt there are many reasons why one would oppose the Roman Catholic Church. One might do so for cultural or racial reasons, seeing Romanism as a foreign influence in Scotland. One might take a stand to protect one's class and social position, with Rome appearing as the champion of unrest among the lower classes. One might do so purely for reasons of ingrained prejudice, opposing that which one's fathers had opposed. No doubt

James Begg was a sinner like other men, but the point must be made that his opposition to the Church of Rome was not a result of ignorant tradition of uninformed prejudice, but of serious study. In order that this point may be made clear and the foundation of his work against Rome established in detail, his longest published work, *A Handbook of Popery* will be examined in this chapter.[1]

The *Handbook* was published in Edinburgh in 1852 and consists of twelve chapters with appendices, and is over 300 pages in length. It was intended by the author to serve as a manual for those engaged in the conflict with Rome, as a tool with which Protestants might be armed in their effort to protect the Protestantism of the United Kingdom, and as a means by which a witness to Roman Catholics might be encouraged. It was published with the Protestant layman in mind and quotes extensively from the official Roman Catholic teaching, particularly from the Council of Trent, with which such laymen might not be familiar.

Chapter I: Begg introduced his subject by showing that Popery was identified in the Scriptures and that various aspects of its past, present, and future progress were predicted by the Word of God. Begg believed it important to affirm that the success or failure of Romanism in any given age was not a matter of surprise to God, but had been spelled out in His Word beforehand.

> We believe it is essential to fix in our minds the truth, that the outline of the actual system of Popery is clearly predicted and sketched in the Word of God, and that nothing has happened, or can happen, in

---

1. James Begg, *A Handbook of Popery: or, Text-Book of Missions for the Conversion of Romanists; Being Papal Rome Tested by Scripture, History, and Its Recent Working.* (Edinburgh: Johnstone & Hunter, 1852). Since all quotations in this chapter will be from this one work, page numbers will be included in the text.

regard to that system, for which we, with the Book of God in our hands, were not bound to be prepared. (p. 11)

The following proofs were put forward by Begg as evidence for his claim.

First, Popery was foretold by the book of Daniel. He quotes Daniel 2:31f. and Daniel 7:2f. as examples.

Second, Paul predicts the growth and offers a description of the nature of Popery as it was to be. Evidence is offered from II Thessalonians 2:3-11 and I Timothy 4:1-4.

Third, John predicted the rise and the overthrow of the Papal system, in passages such as Revelation 13:1-8; 17:9; and chapter 18. (pp. 12-17)

Chapter II: Having asserted that Christians ought not to be surprised at the advance of a system such as Romanism, Begg compared the Church of Rome with primitive Christianity as it is shown to us in the New Testament. Such an analysis revealed that:

whilst … it is of great importance to proceed to the present inquiry with candour, it is necessary to keep in view that Popery, broadly viewed, is a system affording a most striking contrast, in all its essential features, to primitive Christianity. (p. 19)

Chapter III: Begg came to the heart of the matter when he asserted that Popery, not only standing in contrast to the Christianity of the New Testament, was also a corruption of the true rule of faith. The Church of Rome denied the sufficiency of the Word of God as a final arbiter in all matters of religious controversy, and in its place substituted a very different standard of appeal, that of the Church itself. This was far from a minor point of an interesting but insignificant doctrine. The very heart of godliness and the foundation of saving faith is at stake here. Begg believed that the Roman Church stood condemned by the Word of God in three ways:

> First, prophetically; ... second, by special anticipation ... of some of its leading peculiarities and third, by a plain statement of doctrines, obviously opposed to all the essential dogmas of Rome. (p. 29)

By placing the voice of the Church and the Pope above that of the Word, the Roman Church showed itself to be not only ignorant of some conclusion or other to be drawn from scripture, but in direct opposition to truths plainly taught by the Word. There was to be no standard of appeal other than the Word of God, and this truth is taught by the Bible in two ways:

> First, it being admitted that God's revelation to man is the only rule of faith; is there any other revelation of God in the world than the Scriptures of the Old and New Testament contain? The Papist says that there is, viz., the Apocrypha, tradition, decisions of councils, etc. The Protestant affirms that there is not ... (p. 29)

> Secondly, who is to interpret the revelation of God supposing it discovered? The Papist affirms that it is the church, or particularly the priest. The Protestant holds that every man is entitled and bound to interpret the revealed will of God for himself ... (p. 30)

Chapter IV: The Roman Church failed in its attempt to set up a standard of authority apart from the Word of God. It is to be understood, therefore, that having failed in this fundamental area of authority, similar failures were to follow from this in many areas of faith and practice. Begg looked at the Roman doctrine of the Pope as the Vicar of Christ and Head of the Church and saw this as clear evidence that the Romanist was a part of an institution which, in spite of exaggerated claims to the contrary, was not a part of the Church of Christ at all.

> Having now settled, as we believe, that the Scriptures of truth, interpreted by every man for himself, with the promised aid of the Spirit of God, form the only standard of appeal in all questions pertaining to the Christian faith, we now proceed to try the Church of Rome by that infallible standard ... (p. 72)

These false claims of the Roman Church rest upon seven fallacies, each of which can be disproved from Scripture.

(1.) The Roman Church argues that Christ chose Peter to be the head or foundation of the church. Begg showed by an analysis of the biblical passages that such an argument is a misreading of the Scriptures. He questioned the Romanist claim that Peter ministered in Rome, but recognized that even if this claim be accepted by historians and Peter is recognized as the founder of the church at Rome:

> ... it would be impossible to convince us that the triple-crowned monsters who have since reigned there have had the slightest claim to be regarded as his successors. (p.79)

(2.) Much was made by the Roman Church and its defenders of the assumption that the Church of Christ will always have a distinct visible and obvious place in the world as a formal institution. The fact that the institution of the Papacy and of the Roman Church can be traced farther back in history than the various Protestant Churches is therefore seen as an argument in favor of the rightness of the Romanist cause. Begg asserted that this theory operated on the false idea of what the church is to be. It failed to distinguish between the visible and the invisible church.

The institution itself is not the Church of Christ, according to James Begg.

> There may be a large visible church, and very few real Christians in it after all. There may be a very small visible church and yet a number of real Christians, "God's hidden ones," as was [un]doubtedly the case during the bloody persecutions of Papal Rome in the dark ages. (p. 85)

(3.) The Roman Church believed that the apostles committed the truths which they received from Christ to a select group of the faithful, who in turn passed them on to others. Thus, those who stand in the "apostolic succession" are in fact the ministers of the Church of Christ. This teaching can be shown to be false, first, because no such succession, in and of itself would identify the true minister of Christ, even if its existence could be proved. According to Begg, "Judas had not only what is called 'apostolical succession,' he was himself an apostle ..." (p. 89)

(4.) The claim that the visible church of Christ, identified with the Church of Rome, had received a promise that it should in all ages be infallibly guided into all truth is one which Begg cannot find in Scripture. History shows, he argued, that even the most ancient Church, not long after the Ascension of Christ, was already corrupted by various false teachings and practices. (p. 90)

(5.) Miracles are used by the Roman Church as evidence of its claim to be the true Church of Christ. Begg analyzed these supposed miracles and found them to be incredible in most cases. Even though such claims could not always be proved to be false, however,

> ... we are expressly told in the Scripture that wonderful works, if wrought to confirm a falsehood, are of no value. (p. 95)

The Scripture proof given here is Deuteronomy 13:1-5.

(6.) The fact that the Roman Church can point to great numbers, large buildings, and wonderful artistic creations is used to support is claim to be the true Church. But Begg rejected the argument. "Numbers are no test of Truth." If the claim of size, visible strength, and number of adherents be admitted as a means of judging the truth of the claims of any institution, then clearly the heathens themselves have the argument won, for their claims would far excel that of Popery. (p. 96)

(7.) Finally, Begg rejected as a fallacy the Roman Church's claim to truth which was based on her claim to sanctity. Holiness itself might indeed be used as a mark of the Church of Christ, but the sanctity evidenced by Popery was nothing but a subversion of the true religion of the Bible. Further evidence of this claim was offered by Begg in chapter VI of the book where he considered Popery as a subversion of the moral law.

Chapter V: Not only does the Romanist misuse the doctrine of the Church, but the Gospel itself, which ought to be defended by Christ's Church, is attacked and denied by Popery. Begg condemned the Roman Church for its subversion of three basic doctrines of the Gospel.

First, Popery perverts the doctrine of Scripture in regard to sin. This perversion can be seen in the Roman teaching of baptismal regeneration, which makes light of the true corruption of original sin, and its ethical distinction between venial and mortal sins which betrays a lack of appreciation for the majesty of the Holy God. In both these instances, Popery goes beyond the bounds of Scriptural doctrine. (p. 105)

Second, the Scriptural doctrine of justification is subverted by the Roman Church. Begg recognized this doctrine as one of the most significant in the history of the Church, particularly in terms of the Protestant-Roman Catholic debate. He condemned the Romanist teaching which he understood to be an exaltation of works at the expense of faith. (p. 108)

Third, the doctrine of adoption and sanctification is subverted by Romanist teaching. Requirements other than those of Scripture were added to these teachings, while, at the same time, biblical standards of holiness were ignored.

> As Rome knows no church of God but a visible one; she knows of no adoption into God's family, but such as she confesses ... Nothing can be more inconsistent with the truths of Scripture which makes adoption an act of sovereign grace. (p. 110)

The example of Romanist saints serves as Begg's proof of her false teaching. He cited examples of those honored by the Roman Church who apparently followed the Roman doctrines in regard to sin, justification, adoption, and sanctification, but who must be judged, in the light of the Word of God, to have been nothing less than the greatest sinners. The claims of the Church of Rome to doctrinal purity are betrayed by the example of her own sons. (p. 111)

Chapter VI: Begg believed that wrong thinking led to wrong acting, that false doctrine must be followed by false ethics and false living. He considered the doctrine of the Roman Church in chapters V and VI of the *Handbook* and then went on in chapter VII to consider what he terms Popery's systematic overthrow of the whole moral law.

> It may be laid down as a fixed principle, that fallen man has no correct knowledge of true morality, except in so far as he derives it from

the Revelation of God ... Man, besides, cannot practice true morality, except in consequence of an entire renovation of heart wrought by the Holy Spirit. Popery wilfully repudiates both these essential elements. She abjures the Bible as the standard of faith; she denies the Holy Spirit as the only author of true sanctity. (p. 118)

Begg proceeded to convict the Roman Church for violations of each of the Ten Commandments in its teaching and practice.

First Commandment: The command is that we worship only the Lord God, but Popery teaches the worship of others besides God alone.

Now, the Pope himself assumes the names, and accepts the worship of Jehovah; and it is quite certain that Popery has "gods many and lords many." (p. 120)

Begg continued by listing examples from the liturgies and prayer books of the Roman Church which show that false worship had been given to the saints and to Mary.

Second Commandment: After noting that Rome attempts to ignore the significance of this commandment altogether by the amalgamation of the second with the first, Begg states that image-worship was in fact practiced by the Roman Church, quoting from the decrees of the Council of Trent as evidence of this abomination. (p. 129)

Third Commandment: The command to use the Lord's Name rightly and to abstain from blasphemy and perjury is clearly overturned by Rome in the titles given to the Pope, and in the various ways in which Roman priests were encouraged to swear to falsehoods in order to protect the confessional. Numerous examples of such advice are offered in the text. (p. 133)

Fourth Commandment: The command to keep the Sabbath Day is broken by Rome in two ways. First, in the most obvious fashion the Sabbath is not observed in Romanist lands. But just as significantly, the first part of the commandments "six days shalt thou labour ..." is ignored by the poverty of monks and friars who do not earn their livings, and by the great number of saints' days which interfere with honest and lawful labor on days other than the Sabbath. (pp. 141-144) Begg was willing to work for early closing hours for the working man as a part of his social reforms, but he refused to allow idleness particularly when it was cloaked with a false religiosity.

Fifth Commandment: In typical Puritan fashion, Begg saw the fifth commandment as a requirement for men to honor not only their physical parents, but also their social superiors, in particular the civil magistrate. He cited examples of Thomas Becket as one who refused lawful allegiance to the magistrate and argued that the Roman view of the Church's superiority to all civil powers was a violation of God's Law. (p. 147)

Sixth Commandment: The whole history of the Roman Church shows its violation of the commandment which forbids murder. Begg cited the Roman Church's record of persecution following the sentence of excommunication and its acquiescence to murder when admitted to in the confessional as examples. (p. 151)

Seventh Commandment: As in the fourth commandment, so in regard to the seventh, the Roman Church errs in a twofold fashion, first by forbidding to marry where no such command is given in scripture, and secondly, as a result of the unscriptural requirement of celibacy for the clergy, its acceptance of the practice of adultery and fornication (p. 160)

Eighth Commandment: Having discussed the Romanist error of distinguishing venial and mortal sins, Begg cited the relegation of stealing, under certain circumstances, to the category of the venial as an example of Romanist encouragement of violation of the commandments. (p. 174)

Ninth Commandment: False witness was not only accepted by the Roman Church, but, according to James Begg, it was encouraged. This occurs when the advice regarding equivocation and mental reservation in the taking of oaths is seriously followed. He quoted extensively from Romanist writings on this subject to illustrate not only Popery's willingness to excuse that which God's Word calls sin, but its active encouragement of that which is displeasing in His sight. (p. 179)

Tenth Commandment: Begg considered the history of the Roman Church, particularly as it evidenced a desire for temporal power, pomp and worldly majesty, and saw there a clear violation of the commandment against coveting. Where power exists, the Roman Church desires it, and thus betrays its status as a worldly institution rather than the true Church of Christ. (p. 180)

The conclusion which Begg reached as a result of his examination of the teaching and practice of the Roman Church in the light of the Scriptures is obvious: "Thus we have proved that Popery notoriously violates THE WHOLE TEN COMMANDMENTS OF THE LAW OF GOD." (p. 187)

Chapter VII: Not only does Popery violate the Ten Commandments; it also promotes sinful living by its practices of confession, absolution, indulgences, and its doctrine of purgatory.

The requirement that one confess to a priest had become a means of achieving false peace of conscience without true biblical repentance. So, too, the pronouncing of absolutions – the declaration that a man's sins were forgiven in the Name of God – could not help but encourage a false peace in the human heart. The confessional and its absolution, having been separated from the biblical teachings regarding repentance and faith, were used by the Roman Church instead as a means of increasing its worldly power. As such it served its task well, but the tragedy of human souls left in the darkness of their sin without the light of the Gospel, shows that it was a costly way to achieve such an end.

> The proper view of confession is not as a Divine appointment – for it has not a shadow of ground to rest upon in the Divine Word – but as a political device of immense power. The confessional is, in truth, one great pillar of priestly influence. The man who knows the whole secrets of his neighbour's heart and life, is virtually his master. (p. 191)

As it was with the confessional, so it was with the doctrine of purgatory and indulgences. These only encouraged false hope and turned men away from the true hope as it is to be found in Christ.

Chapter VIII: The Papal system, having encouraged sin and vice in men, also subverted the commands and ordinances of the Gospel.

> There are special commands binding upon us ... repentance unto life, faith in the Lord Jesus Christ, the upholding of a standing ministry, the public worship of God, and an observance of the sacraments of the Christian Church. Now, it is easy to prove that Popery deliberately perverts and corrupts all these. (p. 228)

We are commanded by the New Testament to repent, but the Roman Church tells men to do penance. Not only are the words of Scripture such as Matthew 3:2 changed, but the whole meaning and intention of the Word of God is altered. Penance has been substituted for biblical repentance, and Begg could not find such a thing as Romanist penance in the Bible. The danger here was not only that the souls of men were left in sin's bondage, but the grace of God itself was blasphemed.

> [Penance] is not only a pure invention, but a most sinful one, inasmuch as it is fitted to conceal the amazing grace of the Gospel, to disparage the character of God, and to make poor sinners imagine that they can, to a large extent, save themselves. (p. 230)

What made this sin all the worse, according to James Begg, was that it was done for mercenary motives. It was designed to exalt the priesthood, to win gifts from hopeless sinners. The grace of God and a biblically awakened conscience have been put aside as unnecessary and unwanted. (p. 230)

As it was with repentance, so too with faith itself. That which man can do has been substituted for the working of the Holy Spirit. Faith has been tied to the doctrines of the Roman Church, to the workings of the priesthood, to the rituals of the sacramental life. It was far removed from the grace of God in Christ.

> With Papists ... faith is a mere assent of the understanding to statements propounded by the church, however erroneous. They have no idea of it as a closing with the record of the living God, and far less as an act of simple reliance on the omnipotent power of a living Saviour ... (p. 233)

Begg's polemic against the priesthood might be interpreted as mere anti-clericalism, but he made a clear distinction between the practice of the Roman Church and the true biblical doctrine of the ministry. The idea of a sacrificing priesthood was rejected by Begg as foreign to the New Testament. The true minister of Christ was contrasted with the false priest of the Roman Church in terms of the task he sought to perform and the power he used to perform it. Begg quoted from a letter which evidenced all that he saw as despotic in the Romanist claim to priestly power.

> The priests claim the most despotic and arbitrary power over their votaries in all lands. Priest Cahill, in a late letter to the Papists of Liverpool, says, referring to Lord John Russell, – "Let him know that when I choose to address you under the sanction of the church, *I can command you to do what I please, and that you will neither walk, nor drink, nor sing, nor dance, but according to my pleasure!* (p. 245)

Not only was this evidence of the false foundation of the Roman priesthood, but the whole Papal system was shown to be a real factor in affairs in Britain.

> To talk, therefore, of Popery as representing the power merely of an old and feeble man at Rome, is only to betray our own weakness and want of penetration. That old man commands the most powerful and obsequious army in the world. (p. 245)

Along with Popery's corruption of the New Testament ministry was its corruption of biblical worship, particularly in regard to the sacraments. The Roman Church established a new sacramental system, unknown to the New Testament, by reinstituting sacrifice, by offering prayer in an unknown tongue, and by excluding the people from the worship of the Church. The sacraments were corrupted by adding to their number, and by altering the nature of the two of biblical origin. Indeed, the Lord's Supper had been so altered by the Romanists that its nature and identity was made completely unrecognizable. (p. 251)

94

Chapter IX: In this chapter, Begg considered other unscriptural practices of the Roman Church, including the requirement to abstain from eating meat at certain times, the maintenance and worship of relics, the institution of votive offerings and Papal benedictions. Popery was seen by Begg as an enemy of knowledge, both scriptural and scientific, and as an institution which was opposed to human liberty and social progress. (pp. 265-276)

Chapter X: In this chapter, Begg reviewed what he termed "prominent peculiarities of Popery" and showed that these errors had been spoken of in the Scriptures.

Chapter XI: Having offered an analysis of the errors or the Roman Church, Begg dealt in this chapter with the question of its continued progress, particularly with the cause of its increasing power in Great Britain.

To understand the power of the Roman Church, one must first accept the fact that one is dealing with an institution which, in spite of its claims to holiness, is, in Begg's terms, "the most unscrupulous agence ... that ever existed in the world." (p. 301) This was particularly the case when one considered the actions of the Jesuits who were prepared as an order, "to set at defiance every law, human and divine, at the bidding of their superiors, and for the accomplishment of their objects." (p. 301)

The nineteenth century was seen to be a testing time for Great Britain. The Roman Church directed its whole power and policy in an attempt to win influence, if not actual control, of the United Kingdom. In this struggle, Begg noted three elements of success which were commanded by Rome, in addition to its more subtle advantages.

1. The funds of the Propaganda, gathered from the whole world, are largely concentrated at this moment upon Britain ... 2. We have the annual swarm of priests thrown off from our own training school at Maynooth, which single institution receives from Government £30,000 per annum ... 3. As soon as any man or woman of influence is converted to Popery at home of abroad, their whole wealth and position are instantly made available in extending the triumph of Antichrist in this country. (pp. 308-309)

The progress of Popery in the United Kingdom was a matter of concern not only to active members of the Protestant Churches, but to all subjects of the realm who valued human freedom, for the result of any victory for Popery was certain.

We dare not even contemplate such an issue. But when did Rome ever triumph except to introduce not only the overthrow of religion, but the most brutal ignorance and despotism, in so far as the people are concerned? (p. 311)

Romanism was gaining power and influence in the United Kingdom because of what Begg termed internal and external causes. Begg saw the internal cause to be the fallen religiosity of man. (p. 314) Such religiosity found the ritual and dogmas of the Papacy to be of great appeal, for it strengthened the fundamental principle of mankind since the Fall that he is sovereign. Beyond this, however, were the external causes, which Begg identified as the low estate of true, vital religion in the land. This only served the cause of Rome. It was the absence of such true religion in Britain which allowed the practical advantages to be won by the Romanists, mentioned above, along with its clear influence in Parliament, to go unchecked. (p. 316)

Chapter XII: In his final chapter, Begg considered the possibility of a revival of true Reformation spirit in Britain in the face of the Romanist threat. He made four suggestions for achieving this goal:

> 1. A spirit of Christian union should be warmly cherished amongst true Protestants ... 2. The thorough instruction of the people of Britain in regard to the true nature of the Papal system ... 3. We must labour to secure the withdrawal of all public support from the Popish system ... 4. Missions to Papists must be established in all the leading towns of Britain, and in every district of Ireland. (pp. 319-321)

As in his other programs of reform, Begg's hope for the defense of Protestantism in the United Kingdom involved the education of the people, demands for the government to act in accordance with the Establishment Principle and time-honored standards, and the founding of aggressive societies, missions, and pressure groups.

His *Handbook* was not merely an abstract analysis of the Romanist system, but a call for action, a manifesto for Protestant defense. It was the contention of James Begg, in regard to the threat of the advancing power of the Roman Church, as in all other matters of interest to his public career as a minister of the Free Church of Scotland, that true biblical godliness ought to lead to concerted actions. It was the cause of mobilizing and instructing those engaged in such actions that James Begg saw as his life's work.

Chapter IV

BEGG AND THE HISTORIANS

HISTORY has not been kind to James Begg. The general opinion is that while he may have had some redeeming qualities, an overall evaluation of his career reveals that which is unattractive and unworthy of emulation. His work of social reform is usually recognized as the one area where Begg did contribute something of worth to the ecclesiastical history of Scotland.

The source of this interpretation of Begg's life and work can be found in the biography of Robert Rainy by Patrick Carnegie Simpson, published in 1909. Simpson stressed the ability and power of James Begg. He described him as a man of great natural powers and a born leader. Begg was recognized by Simpson as a moving speaker, one who was able to sway public opinion by the power of the spoken word. But having said these positive things, Simpson went on to deal a very negative conclusion. Begg was a man out of touch with his own day. His views were not those of his time. Simpson evaluates his theological foundation as follows:

From the fact that he was hopelessly narrow in his theology and opposed to every kind of progress, people are apt to think he was only ignorant. And he was ignorant in the literary sense. It must also be admitted that he was not a man built on refined ethical lines.[1]

If this was the view of Simpson, then he built it upon the foundation laid by Rainy himself. In response to a request of twenty years before, Rainy had offered this evaluation of his great opponent in the Free Church.

> Begg was the evil genius of the Free Church. He introduced a policy of conspiracy and of attempting to carry points by threatening us with law. No man did more to lower the tone of the Church and to secularize it.[2]

This quotation was to find its way into many histories of the nineteenth century Free Church up to and including those of the present time.

The same accusations were made by J.R. Fleming in 1927. He tried to give Begg his due from the start by suggesting that his work of social reform was worthy of praise.

> We shall be obliged as this narrative proceeds to set forth the unlovely aspects of Begg's later career as an ecclesiastic. Justice has not yet been done to his earlier and more beneficial work as a tribune of the people and an eloquent champion of reforms in the State, rightly regarded by him as vital in the interests of morality and religion. Had he continued to lead along those lines, his name would have been more honoured in Scotland to-day than it is. Let us not grudge a belated tribute to what he endeavoured to do and actually achieved.[3]

---

1. Patrick Carnegie Simpson, *The Life of Principal Rainy*. (London: Hodder & Stoughton, 1909), Vol. I, p. 198.
2. Ibid., Vol. II, p. 50.
3. Fleming, p. 150.

These "unlovely aspects" become clear in Fleming's analysis of the Voluntary Controversy. He stated at the beginning that the minority who stood against Union with the United Presbyterians held a view of Union which was "absorption in the interests of their own exclusive dogmas."[4] This minority was unwilling to move toward a new goal, which Fleming describes as:

> ... a comprehensive Church based on essential catholic truth, with wide freedom to hold individual opinions on matters not entering into the substance of the faith.[5]

It was this minority, which could not precept such a revolutionary concept, which Begg molded into an articulate party in the Free Church. He became "the champion of the obscurantist and ultra-conservative elements in the Church."[6]

Perhaps the best indication of Fleming's opinion of James Begg can be seen in his vision of what the Free Church of Scotland might have been if the crisis of 1900 had occurred in 1873 instead, and Begg and his party had left the Free Church to the pro-Union majority.

> Undoubtedly a Church litigation that in its results would in all probability have anticipated the history of 1904-5. Possibly, though one cannot be sure of this, a different ending to the Disestablishment agitation that lay ahead. Robertson Smith might have been retained in his professorship. Events would certainly have moved more rapidly in a progressive direction. But we are inclined to think that the check which came just when it did was proof that Scotland was not at

---

4. Ibid., p. 175.

5. Ibid., p. 175.

6. Ibid., p. 180.

this time prepared for a positive and fruitful movement in the field of Church unity. Another generation had to pass ere the growing sense of catholicity could overcome the forces of sectarian prejudice.[7]

Writing in 1960, Stewart Mechie devoted a whole chapter of his book on Scottish social development to James Begg and the housing question. This is probably one of the only serious attempts to deal with Begg on the part of a professional historian in the present era. Mechie is generally sympathetic to Begg's work of reform, giving him credit for his labors on behalf of the working class. His analysis of Begg leads him to conclude that in spite of his conservative temperament, he held radical opinions, and had a deep sympathy with the common people. Mechie calls him "something of a demagogue,"[8] but is clearly attracted to him as a reformer.

In the 1970's Andrew Drummond and James Bulloch produced two fine works on the Church in Victorian Scotland. Naturally, James Begg is mentioned often in these volumes. The basic evaluation of Begg is that he was "conservative to the end and out of touch with their age."[9]

Specifically, these authors note two problems with Begg and his social reforms. First, they condemn his anti-Romanism.

A steady stream of propaganda against the Roman Church, viewed with suspicion by most Protestants but supported by an occasional minister like Begg, continued and its counterpart is the bitterness and resentment which it aroused in some Roman Catholics. Begg was a man whose strong sympathy with the poor and oppressed

---

7. Ibid., p. 187.

8. Mechie, p. 135

9. Drummond & Bulloch, *Victorian Scotland*, p. 197.

might have led him to think kindly of the immigrants, but he was fiercely anti-Romanist and Roman Catholics in turn completely misunderstood him.[10]

The second accusation which Drummond and Bulloch make against Begg is that he was limited in his approach to reform and was unable to reach the lower classes, being concerned only with the middle and working classes of society. The authors distinguish this from what they consider to be the liberal's concern for all the people.

One view which Begg espoused does come in for a share of credit here. That was his dream of a national Church. In spite of what others might conclude, these authors believe that Begg had a vision for the Church in Scotland which was worthy of praise.

> Begg ... was regarded by his opponents as truculent and obstinate, an intriguer and a demagogue, but one of formidable ability. Begg had retained a rugged Calvinism which the new men found distasteful; he still retained the tradition of a National Church, free and inclusive, while they had begun to settle for a denominational outlook ...[11]

Drummond and Bulloch are willing to give Begg his due. They recognize, however, that many who have studied the nineteenth century history of the Scottish Church have been negative in their evaluation of him.

> It would be hard to find a better example of that misunderstood type of Free Church minister whom posterity has disliked and whose merits have been forgotten. Begg fought as resolutely for

10. Ibid., p.74.
11. Ibid., p. 323.

a declining Calvinist theology as he did for justice to the underdog and the victim of a harsh society because – for him – the two causes were intimately related. He stood firmly for the principles and the prejudices of the Disruption Fathers and carried into a strange new world an intransigence which led him, in the end, to commit himself to lost causes.[12]

Thus far, this is the final word on James Begg: a man of principle, an advocate of social reform, a champion of lost causes. The tragedy of James Begg, from the viewpoint of the historians, is that the principles which he defended were not those of the progressive forces of his day. His social concern was not able to confine itself to acceptable reforms; he insisted on opposing Romanism with as much vigor as he did poor housing and seat rents. The causes he championed may have been noble and great at one time, but the judgment of history is that by Begg's day they were merely outworn anachronisms.

Perhaps, for all his faults in their minds, Begg is worthy of respect for at least one achievement. Drummond and Bulloch recognize him as one of the few men of his age who was able to frustrate the plans of Robert Rainy. It says something of the strength of the man, that he was able to do so, not merely while he was living, but long after his death. The great events of the Free Church case in 1903 could be seen as being presided over by the ghost of James Begg.

The historians have done their work on James Begg and an analysis of their labors reveals that they found much that was unfavorable in the man. They have opposed his theology as out-

---

12. Ibid., p. 186.

dated Calvinism. They have rejected his methods as an attempt to stifle the modern trends in the Free Church of Scotland in the interest of an ever-declining minority. But all the while they recognize and honor his social conscience. Can the reason for this be that Begg is not so much the subject of their evaluation as the principles which motivated him? Simpson, Fleming, Drummond and Bulloch did not accept the Calvinism which Begg preached, therefore they have criticized him for preaching it. They did not approve of the cause of the minority in the Free Church, therefore they condemn him for leading the fight on behalf of that minority. Only in the social realm are these twentieth century historians able to accept the principle which motivated James Begg, so it is that only here were they able to find that which can be approved and supported. When all is said and done, perhaps the judgment of the historians is not so much an evaluation of James Begg as it is a judgment of the historians themselves and their views of what is right and proper and Christian. As they attempt such a judgment and evaluation, the works of James Begg force them to deal with his theology, his views on government of Church and State, as well as his social opinions. Perhaps he would have been pleased with this and considered it something of a victory. The historians rightly judge that Begg cannot be separated from Calvinism, the Establishment Principle, and anti-Romanism. For this reason they criticize the man, for they believe such principles to be false. But what if the principles are true? Then Begg becomes a stalwart hero instead of an outdated advocate of lost causes.

Conclusion

AT the beginning of this study, it was put forward that an examination of the writings of James Begg might be of some interest, first in their own right, as honoring to one who labored for the cause of Christ in his day; secondly, as a means of asking again some basic questions about the Church-State relation; and thirdly, as an attempt to learn about the Free Church of Scotland and the reasons for its rapid decline from the orthodoxy of the Disruption Fathers. While many questions remain unanswered, nevertheless some conclusions can be drawn in each of these areas.

In spite of the views of Rainy and the historians, Begg does appear to be a character of some personal attraction and worth. The "evil genius" appears instead to be a man of principle. Indeed, he was one who was willing to sacrifice a great deal for the cause of conscience and principle. In this he must be understood as a contrast to those who have little by way of principle and always labor in the realm of the pragmatic. But Begg is just as much a contrast to those who have great ideals and principles, but do nothing about them. Whatever else he may have been, James Begg was a man of action.

It is significant that many historians recognize Begg's qualities of leadership and his ability in public speaking. Rainy accused him of bringing a spirit of faction into the Free Church and many have agreed with that accusation. But Begg's ability to direct the minority in the Free Church, his willingness to use the accepted means of parliamentary debate, and his determination to appeal to the civil courts if necessary in the Voluntary Controversy; all these are not properly understood if seen only as inconvenient stumbling blocks to the proposed Union with the United Presbyterians. Certainly Rainy saw them in this way. But a better approach would be to say that just as Begg claimed that all aspects of life, public and private, were subject to the Word of God and were to be won for the Gospel, so too, he was obligated to use all his talents for that cause. Public oratory, leadership skills, and knowledge of the civil law were talents which Begg was willing to place in his Master's service.

Finally, by way of personal evaluation, it should be noted that Begg was one who was willing to draw the conclusions that others shunned. No doubt many in the Free Church in the early 1870's recognized that their principles were such that, unless the pro-Union majority was willing to slacken the pace, a secession was required. Many may have recognized this, but Begg was willing to act in an intelligent and organized fashion to deal with it. He was prepared to carry out the task. The demands of his own conscience, the principles of the Disruption Fathers, the great causes which James Begg revered, all those required such action. Begg was unwilling to allow pragmatic considerations to turn him from the goal. To others, who were unwilling to act in this way, Begg's activities looked like divisiveness, but to one who accepted the principles involved they were the logical conclusion, the necessary consequence, indeed the only path for one of Christian conscience.

In regard to the Establishment Principle, it must be said that it is an issue largely ignored by modern Reformed Christians, particularly in the United States. This is understandable, of course, in the light of the traditional interpretation of the Constitution which requires separation of Church and State. But would we not do well to look again? Does not Begg show us the great danger of allowing our view of the civil power to be one of neutrality in matters of the Gospel? Perhaps it is time to read once more those revisions to the Westminster Confession accepted by the American Presbyterian Churches. Does it really call upon us to allow our government to operate as an institution free from any demand of the Law of God? Begg argues clearly that such a view is unacceptable to the Christian. The fear of an Anglican Establishment in the newly formed nation was enough to make the provision for the Bill of Rights prohibiting the establishment of a Church by the Congress acceptable to non-episcopal Churches. Was not too much given away? Was not the alliance with the free thinkers, Secularists, Deists, and other non-Christians of the period an unfortunate result? It is no doubt too late now, after two hundred years of constitutional development, to return and start again. Certainly the Reformed Churches of orthodox belief are so much in the minority that they would have little to say even if such a re-evaluation were possible. But perhaps the example of Begg may show us that something at least is possible. We can begin to deal with the civil government as an institution under the authority of the Word of God. We can begin to tell our leaders so, to state clearly the demands and implications of that Word for the conduct of public life. It may be that few will listen. But the work of James Begg teaches us that the relative size of support for any league is never a true means of judging the rightness of that cause.

The reasons for the decline of the Free Church cannot be definitively analyzed even through an examination of the career of James Begg. It is a subject worthy of serious study. Historians of the modern Reformed Churches would do well to examine and learn from this tragedy. Nevertheless, some points can be made as a result of this study.

It is clear that the principles of the Free Church of Scotland were not agreed upon by all within the denomination. It would appear that the personal influence of men like Chalmers having been removed, there was no force of unity left in the Church. The work of James Begg in his opposition to the Voluntary Movement shows clearly that even in regard to such a basic principle as this, no unanimous voice was to be heard from the Free Church. This was not merely in regard to an academic principle which had little effect on practical matters, but, as Drummond and Bulloch have pointed out, the whole question of whether the Free Church of Scotland was to be a National Church or just another denomination was at stake. It is significant that it was only thirty years after the Disruption that the Church almost divided once more on this issue.

Another point of significance can be seen in the fact that the Conservative party in the Free Church seemed to be unsure of the course it wished to take. Perhaps what was missing was a master plan, an all encompassing goal for the Constitutionalists. Without such a plan of vision, all they could do was to respond to the various attacks made by the liberal, pro-Union party. The agenda for the debates in the Free Church was clearly set by the majority.

Perhaps the best way to describe this problem is to say that when the conservatives were strong, they were unwilling to leave the Church; when they were weak, they seemed unable to organize themselves to do so.

There are lessons to be learned from the events of this period, lessons of importance to modern conservative Presbyterians, whether struggling still in large liberal Churches or in the smaller, more orthodox denominations.

First, the struggle must be fought on the basic issues. Whenever a threat is made against a matter of biblical or confessional truth, it must be dealt with. There must be organization and proper leadership. The events of 1872 show that a minority organized for a specific fight on a clearly defined purpose can carry great weight.

Secondly, the conservatives must recognize that the time may come when separation is required. Certainly, Begg and his followers knew this. But their views were quickly forgotten. The conservatives were prepared in 1893 as they had been in 1872, but they would not carry out the obviously required step when the Declaratory Act became the law of the Church. What was missing was the quality of leadership so evident in the earlier period by the career of James Begg.

Thirdly, as a clear corollary to the above point, leadership must be cultivated in more than one individual. Begg offered himself to the Conservative cause in the Free Church and did great things on its behalf, but where were the other leaders, the younger men who should have been trained to take over the responsibility when Begg could no longer do so? The absence of effective leadership in the 1880's and 1890's was to be a great want on the part of the conservative forces.

Finally, it should be said that the conservative forces needed to admit the obvious when it appeared before them. Not all in the Free Church agreed on the principles which Begg and his followers held dear. I believe that this points to Begg's greatest failure. It is not enough merely to state the great principles which motivate one to action. Begg often appeared to believe that having quoted from the Confession or from the Reformers or from the Disruption Fathers, or even from the Bible itself, that all was safe. He failed to recognize that many in the Free Church no longer cared what these sources had to say – they had gone beyond such standards. In this sense, perhaps it is true that Begg was a supporter of lost causes. The lost causes were not just the Establishment Principle or anti-Romanism or a national view of the Church; the great lost cause which Begg defended throughout his life was the confessional nature of the Church of Christ. He never put it that way; perhaps he never really recognized the problem, for it was a matter far greater than any specific question of law or interpretation of the Confession on this point or other. Begg operated on the assumption that the Church possessed a foundation which was above the whims of the moment, that was superior to the demands of the age. In this he was at odds with his brethren in the Free Church of Scotland who had already begun to see the structure, the government, the operations of the Church as the true source of unity for the denomination rather than the confessional standards of what the Church believed. The historical judgment must be that in holding such a view Begg was definitely in the minority and was out of touch with the Free Church of his day. The theological judgment as to the rightness or wrongness of such a view is another matter altogether.

When both strengths and weaknesses are listed, when his victories and defeats are catalogued, it must be said that Begg was a worthy heir of the Scottish Presbyterian tradition. He had often viewed the old banner in New Monkland, carried by his forefathers at Bothwell Bridge. The motto was the Covenanters' motto but it serves for James Begg: "For Church and State, According to the Word of God and the Covenant." The Latin was Scotland's motto, but it is uniquely appropriate for James Begg, *"Nemo me impune lacessit."* The picture on the banner was out of the past, from a day when swords were real weapons and blood had to be shed. But Begg, too, carried a dagger and attempted to use it for his cause. His dagger was not the sword of Bothwell Bridge, but "the Sword of the Spirit, which is the word of God."

Select Bibliography

Part I
WORKS OF JAMES BEGG

Free Church Presbyterianism in the United Kingdom: Its Principles, Duties, and Dangers. Edinburgh: Duncan Grant, 1865.

Free Church Principles since the Disruption. Edinburgh: James Nichol, 1869.

A Handbook of Popery; or, Text-Book of Missions for the Conversion of Romanists: Being Papal Rome Tested by Scripture, History, and Its Recent Working. Edinburgh: Johnstone & Hunter, 1852.

Happy Homes for Working Men, and How to Get Them. London: Cassell, Petter, & Galpin; and Edinburgh: James Nichol, 1866.

The Late Dr Chalmers on the Establishment Principle and Irish Protestantism ... Edinburgh: James Nichol, 1868.

Memorial with the Opinions of Eminent Counsel in regard to the Constitution of the Free Church of Scotland. Edinburgh: Johnstone, Hunter & Co., 1874.

Present Aspect of the Union Question. Edinburgh: Ballantyne & Co., 1870.

The Principles, Position, and Prospects of the Free Church of Scotland. Edinburgh: Lyon & Gemmell, 1875.

The Proposed Disestablishment of Protestantism in Ireland: Its Bearings upon the Religion and Liberties of the Empire. Edinburgh: James Nichol, 1868.

Reasons Why No Seat-Rents should be in the Free Church. Edinburgh: John Johnstone, 1843.

The Seat-Rent Question. Edinburgh: John Johnstone, 1839.

Seat Rents brought to the Test of Scripture, Law, Reason, and Experience ... Edinburgh: John Johnstone. 1838.

The Union Question. Edinburgh: James Nichol, 1868.

A Violation of the Treaty of Union the Main Origin of our Ecclesiastic Divisions and Other Evils. Edinburgh: Johnstone, Hunter & Co., 1871.

Voluntaryism Indefensible; or, a Nation's Duty and Right to Profess and Practice Christianity. Edinburgh: no date.

Part II
OTHER WORKS

Bannerman, James. *The Church of Christ*. 2 vols. Edinburgh: The Banner of Truth Trust, 1974.

Burleigh, J.H.S. *A Church History of Scotland*. London: Oxford University Press, 1960.

Collins, G.N.M. *The Heritage of Our Fathers*. Edinburgh: Knox Press, 1974.

Cunningham, William. *Discussions on Church Principles*. Edinburgh: T. & T. Clark, 1863.

Drummond, Andrew & Bulloch, James. *The Church in Late Victorian Scotland, 1874-1900*. Edinburgh: The Saint Andrew Press, 1978.

_____. *The Church in Victorian Scotland, 1843-1874*. Edinburgh: The Saint Andrew Press, 1975.

Fleming, J.R. *The Church in Scotland, 1842-1874*. Edinburgh: T. & T. Clark, 1927.

History of the Free Presbyterian Church of Scotland, 1893-1970. Inverness: J.G. Eccles, no date.

Mechie, Stewart. *The Church and Scottish Social Development, 1780-1870*. London: Oxford University Press, 1960.

Macleod, John. *Scottish Theology in relation to Church History since the Reformation*. Edinburgh: The Banner of Truth Trust, 1974.

Publication Committee of the Free Presbyterian Church of Scotland. *The Confession of Faith* ... Inverness; Eccleslitho, 1970.

Shaw, Robert. *The Reformed Faith*. Inverness: Christian Focus Publications, 1974.

Simpson, Patrick Carnegie. *The Life of Principal Rainy*. 2 vols. London: Hodder & Stoughton, 1909.

Smith, Thomas. *Memoirs of James Begg, D.D., Minister of Newington Free Church, Edinburgh*. Edinburgh: James Gemmell, 1885 & 1888.

Tallach, Ian R. "God's Church in Relation to the State." *The Bulwark* (November/December 1979): 7-17.

Wright, Ronald Selby. *Fathers of the Kirk: Some Leaders of the Church in Scotland from the Reformation to the Reunion*. London: Oxford University Press, 1960,

Index

117

#0063 - 040718 - C0 - 210/148/7 - PB - DID2239980